The Mad Fisherman

Kick Some BASS

with America's Wildest TV Host

St. Martin's Press

New York

The Mad Fisherman

Charlie Moore

with Charles Salzberg

www.stmartins.com

Design by Susan Walsh

Library of Congress Cataloging-in-Publication Data Available upon Request

ISBN-13: 978-0-312-37472-3
ISBN-10: 0-312-37472-0

First Edition: April 2008

10 9 8 7 6 5 4 3 2 1

This book is dedicated to my wife, Angela, and my three wonderful children, Anthony, Nikolas, and Kaitlin. I also dedicate this book to all of those who are willing to sacrifice it all to reach their dreams.

Contents

Acknowledgments

My Family—Daniel Moore, Helen Moore, Danny Moore, David Moore; Christopher, Colleen, Alexandra, and Taylor Moore; Juliana, Madison, and Cameron Compare; Dick and Bonnie Latini; Christine, Bill, Eric, Danny, Emily, and Rebecca Tinkler; Rick, Laura, Zachary, Jake, and Megan Latini; Bass Master Bobby Latini; Alighieri and Mary Latini. I love you all very much. Angela, I, and the kids thank you for all of your support. Bob and Carolyn Sylvester and family; Carmella Moore; Duwane and Shannon Miller; Ted Ancher and family (Thanks for being such a big help with my career. Angela and I love you, Ted.); Doug Orr and family; John Martin and family; Pat Gamere and family; Eric Scharmer and family; Jim Kevlik and family; John "Top Water" Sloan and family; Dennis Reardon and family; Drew Santabarbara; Peter Gold and family and all of my friends at Gold, Orluk & Partners; Ryan Moore and family; Jon Lee; Dustin (Rusty); Chris and Alison Martins; Joel St. Germain and family; Sean Marzerka and family; Sal Malguarnera; Mike Cole; Johnny Cacciatore; Sean McGrail; Harry Sinden; all of my friends and colleagues at NESN; David Parzialle; all my friends at Web-sites.com; Gary Funchion and family; all of my friends at 3B Media and Line 21; the entire Aubuchon family; Chuck and Pat Clement; Mike Mattson; Paul Riley and family; Ernie Boch Jr. and family; Craig Gaunya and family; Steve Talarico and family; Bob Werner and family; Herb Reed; Tom Carpi; George Carey and family;

Larry Saggese and family; Nicki Saggese; Steve Saggese; George Ferullo and family; Larry Piretti and family; Rickey Medlocke; Todd Rucci and family; Charles Salzberg; Mike O'Malley and family; Keith Kevlik; John Leone; Stephen Holmes; Tommy "The Revere Elf" Vaudo; Mike Keane; and Steve Lemoine. To all of the people that we miss dearly: My grandparents, my Uncle Spero Varfis, my good friend John Naramore, and my high school football coach John Carratu. I would also like to thank all of my sponsors and guests. If it weren't for you there would be no show to tape and no story to tell or book to write.

My family: Nikolas, me, Anthony, Kaitlin, and Angela.

My mom, Helen.

The Mad Fisherman

Introduction

'm nervous today. Very nervous. And that's not like me. I never get nervous. Ever.

But tonight is different. Tonight I'm going to the Boston Garden. Sure, I've been to the Garden before. Lots of times. But tonight's a different story. Tonight, I'm going in a stretch limousine, one of six filled with twenty-five people in all. But first, all twenty-five of us are having dinner at Morton's Steakhouse, one of my all-time favorite restaurants. My friend, Ernie Boch Jr., who owns a bunch of car dealerships, will be there. Yes, I'll be getting a Ferrari soon. Ernie, expect a call. Chuck Clement, owner of Eastern Propane and Oil, will be there, as will George Carey, owner of Finz Restaurant, Paul Riley, from Post Woodworking Sheds, and the whole Aubuchon Hardware family—Aubuchon is the title sponsor of my show. And, of course, my entire family. Wouldn't want to forget them.

Tonight is different. I'm being honored at the Boston Garden, home of the Boston Celtics and the Boston Bruins. Tonight, between periods of the hockey game—Go Bruins!—I'm being inducted into the New England Sports Museum in a program called "Gone Fishing: New England's Famous Outdoorsmen." I'm going to be inducted along with Curt Gowdy and Ted Williams. Can you believe it? Me. Charlie Moore. The Mad Fisherman. My name is going to be spoken in the same breath as Curt

Gowdy, one of the greatest sports announcers of all time, and Ted
Williams . . . I don't have to tell you who Ted Williams is, do I?
Does the last .400 hitter in baseball ring a bell?

No wonder I'm nervous. As much as I have an ego—and you
don't need a magnifying glass to find it—I'm still very grounded.
I don't take myself too seriously. But this, well, this is . . . serious.

As you can probably tell by now, tonight is a very big deal for
me. Curt Gowdy Jr. will be there, as well as a representative for
Ted Williams. And then there's my family: my wife, Angela, my
three kids, Anthony, Nikolas, and Kaitlin, and all the people who
helped make my shows—*Charlie Moore Outdoors* and *Beat Charlie
Moore*—wildly successful. Bob Sylvester, my producer, who had a
big part in working with Dick Johnson from the Sports Museum,
will be there, too.

It's been twelve years since I started down this road, but I feel
like my career is just beginning. I'm looking forward to the next
twelve years which, believe me, are going to be even better than
the first ones. But, as for tonight, I told them I wanted the ceremony to be short. Very short. I don't want this to be a long,
drawn-out affair. My stomach couldn't take it.

I, Charlie Moore, will be honored in the Boston Garden. How
could I possibly have imagined all this twelve years ago, when I
was dead broke, married with two kids and another on the way,
and living in my in-laws' house? Well, I probably did imagine it.
But it was just a dream, then. Tonight, it's going to be a reality.

I'm not one for reminiscing about milestones. Heck, I don't
think I've accomplished anything near what I'm going to before
I'm done. It's great to look back and think, "Hey, that was terrific," but that's not what I'm all about. I love what I do. I know
what I have. I know who I am. I know what's important to me.

But how did I get here? How did I get to the point where all
these people are going to be in the stands applauding as I join the
ranks of the true immortals?

And so, while there's still nobody else around, while I'm

waiting nervously for tonight's ceremony, I'll light up an Avo, my favorite brand of cigar, and I'll think about my life and my show, where I've been, how I got there, and where I'm going.

Sit back, my friends, because we're headed over choppy waters . . .

I'm Gonna Get My Own
TV Show. . . . No. Really. I Am.

Here I am in Beverly, Massachusetts, twenty-four years old, two kids, another one on the way, and it's time to cut bait. Time to walk away from a spectacularly unsuccessful attempt at opening my own tackle store. I am, by any measure, an absolute failure. A flop. A bust. On the bright side, I've got nowhere to go but up. At least that's what I tell myself. Because if I don't go up, my friends, I'll go belly up.

But who am I, exactly, and why did I ever think I could possibly make a living selling lures and bait? To really understand me and my success, you've got to accept that some things can't be taught at any university. My theory? You're just born and bred knowing them. At least that's how it was for me.

Please Allow Me to Introduce Myself . . .

First off, my name's Charlie Moore. But you already know that because it's in big letters on the cover of this book, along with my picture. And if you didn't know who I was before you

Me as a kid.

bought this book, you will now. Trust me.

My mom and dad were Southerners. My dad is from Virginia and my mom is from Washington, D.C., where they met. My dad worked in the banking industry in the Treasury building where my mom was a secretary.

My mother's family is from Albania. They are Greek, so we grew up in the Greek Orthodox church. My father's father, who was born and raised in Virginia, was a very tough guy who didn't show his emotions. My dad used to tell me how much my grandfather loved freshwater fishing. He regaled me with stories about my grandfather fishing off a bridge on the Chesapeake. And my grandfather on my mother's side, Papoo, used to tell stories about how he dove for sponges and speared fish for his family. So, it doesn't take a genius to figure out why I've always loved the water and the outdoors.

By the time I showed up on the scene, my family had moved to Lynnfield, Massachusetts. I was the fourth child, and fourth boy (my parents would try it one more time and finally get it right: a girl.) There's Danny, David, Christopher, me, and Juliana. My father was a successful businessman who owned a smoke shop and convenience store. We lived pretty well: a beautiful house, a couple of cars, the whole nine yards.

My father was always intrigued by the Civil War, so much so that growing up I didn't know if my father was Dan Moore or Robert E. Lee. During show-and-tell at school I'd be afraid that the door would smash open and Dad would ride in on a horse, dressed as a confederate general. And I'd be scarred for life. That's the reason I never asked him to come in for show-and-tell. If you think I'm kidding, think again.

Take the vacations we took when I was a kid. We'd jump in the Griswold family station wagon and, without exception, we'd end up at yet another Civil War battlefield. "For the love of God, Dad, can't we go somewhere else for a change? Like Disney World?"

The first time I saw my dad out on one of those battlefields I got out of the station wagon and asked, "Gee, Dad, when does the war start?"

"Oh, no, son, the war was over more than a hundred years ago."

"I don't see any troops coming over the ridge. Should I fire the cannons?"

"I said it already happened, a long time ago."

"Maybe if you'd stopped and asked for directions like Mom said, we'd have gotten here in time."

So those were our family vacations. Going to Pennsylvania. Going to Virginia. Going to the battlefield. Any battlefield.

My dad was like a Southern field general and to understand me and my success, you've got to understand the mind-set of the field general. He doesn't lose. He does everything, at any and every cost, to win. That's how I grew up. When you played football, you played to win, whether it was a pickup game, Pop Warner, or high school.

My father didn't talk much. Didn't have to. His eyes said it all. You'd look over at him and he'd peer right through you as if you weren't there, as if he was only thinking about the upcoming battle and what part you'd play in it. He was a powerful man who could manipulate anybody into doing whatever he wanted you to do. As with any general, if you weren't going to help win the war, you weren't going to be part of the battle. You didn't get anywhere near the front. You were sent back home. No Purple Heart. No nothing. Either you fought his way or you didn't fight at all. That's the way I grew up. Everything was done by my dad's rules. And if you didn't do it his way, he wouldn't even talk to you.

My dad would not accept failure and, in fact, he wouldn't even discuss it. He didn't scream and smack you around. He didn't have to. You just knew what was expected of you. And you did it.

You went to a football game, you played football. And that's where you were supposed to leave the game, on the field. A lot of my success can be traced directly to my dad's personality. One of the reasons my father and I have argued so much over the years is because we're very similar.

In contrast to my father, my mom is bubbly, friendly, outgoing, and very talkative. I share several traits with my mom, one of which is, we both lie about our age. She's always telling the story about how when she went to the doctor he said, "I cannot believe your age." Only trouble is, she's been telling that same story for ten years now. I've lied so much about my age, sometimes I don't even know how old I really am.

The bottom line is, I do business like my dad, while in personality, I'm more like my mom.

As if we in the Moore family needed any more proof, my dad solidified his position as Field General Moore one Christmas Eve not long ago when his current wife, Mrs. Miller—I call her Minnie—officially certified his position. I walked into the living room of their house and came face-to-face with a painting of my dad dressed as General Lee, sitting on a horse. I shook my head, turned to Angela, and said, "That just about sums up my childhood."

Thankfully, he didn't have that painting done until we grew up; otherwise, you can be damn sure we would have lugged that sucker into school for show-and-tell.

Overall, I had a pretty normal childhood, considering who my father was. I liked sports. I loved football.

My older brother Chris was a terrific football player and went on to play in college. He was also captain of the football team. I would have followed in his footsteps, but it didn't work out. I was always in Chris's shadow, working tirelessly just to catch up. But he would always be five years older, so I would always be the tortoise to his hare. That just drove me harder, though.

My senior year on the Lynnfield
Pioneers high school football team (1987).

In many ways, we were polar opposites. Chris is quiet, laid-back. I'm in your face. I'm the one talking smack in between plays. Truth is, if we could have taken the best parts of him and the best parts of me, we would have made a Super Moore, the greatest football player ever. At least that's my version of the story.

So instead, of becoming an All-American quarterback at Boston College, I wound up working with my father in his store, selling cigars and lottery tickets. I'd worked in that store ever since I was a little kid. I'd even set up my own store-within-the-store where I would sell bubble gum and baseball cards, until I graduated to cigars and lottery—I was always a salesman at heart.

By the time I turned eighteen, I was already a successful entrepreneur, the personification of the American Dream. I drove a nice car, ate at nice restaurants, wore nice clothes. My goals were loftier than anyone I knew. I was driven to succeed, just like my father. I've always believed that people are born that way. I don't think you have to go to college to learn how to be an entrepreneur.

Don't get me wrong, there are obviously lots of things you can learn in college. There are certainly things you can learn about being a success in business. But that drive, that ambition, doesn't come from learning about profit-and-loss statements and returns on investment. Self-made people just have that fire inside them, and I always knew I was going to develop into something special. If I worked hard enough at it.

The Day My Life Changed Forever

It was June 27, 1988, the year I turned eighteen. I'd decided to take a day off to relax and chill out, fishing in the ocean with my friends. But at the last minute, and I thank dumb luck for this, I changed my mind and decided that, instead of going with them, I'd rent a favorite—*The Godfather*. So, I headed out to the video store. On the way, I passed a CVS and figured I'd stop in for some Twizzlers to eat while I watched the movie.

I went in and, whoa, there she was behind the counter. The minute I saw her, I forgot all about Twizzlers. All I cared about was this gorgeous girl working the cash register behind the counter. I would have bought something, but in that case I'd have no excuse to hang around. And, believe me, I wanted to hang around that store as long as I possibly could. So, I just stood there, staring at the candy display, sneaking glances at this beautiful girl, looking like a complete idiot.

Finally, she looked at me and said, "It's a tough decision, isn't it?"

"Yeah," I said, mustering my confidence. "But what I really want is behind the counter. What time do you get off?"

"Around six," she said.

So I came back later, and took Angela Latini down to the beach. We just talked and got to know each other. It didn't take long before I knew she was something special.

Angela and I never partied. Instead, I took her to nice restaurants, or we just hung out. We became good friends, and that was very cool. I remember driving up to New Hampshire, where we live now, and we'd cruise through all the nice neighborhoods and look at all the expensive houses that lined the street.

I'd say, "I want that one."

And Angela would say, "I want that one."

And then we'd talk about what *our* house would be like.

But our courtship wasn't all wine and roses. I have a great relationship with my in-laws now, but in the beginning my mother-in-law and I would go at it. It was pretty bad there for a while.

At one point, I wasn't even allowed in the house.

I don't think Angela's mom, Bonnie, had anything against me personally; she was just frightened about losing her daughter and didn't want to let her go. The funny thing was, we weren't even out drinking or partying. I never did drugs, either. Maybe her mother was scared by how driven I was. Even at that age. Hell, at

Angela and me at her senior prom (1989).

Me and my first Corvette (1995).

eighteen I was driving around in a brand-new Corvette—besides working for my father, I had a second job selling Corvettes. Her daughter was coming home with Gucci bags, we were going to fancy restaurants for dinner. It must have looked like all I cared about was making a lot of money.

That's the funny part, looking back on it. Usually, guys get in trouble with a girl's parents because they do drugs, or because they take their daughter to wild parties. Not me. I just wanted to be president of the United States.

It all came to a head the day Angela graduated from North Shore Community College, in the spring of 1991. Not only wasn't I allowed in the house, I was forbidden to attend the graduation ceremony.

But we were in love with each other, so that wasn't going to stop me. I would be at graduation whether her parents wanted me there or not. Of course, I couldn't sit with the family, so I found a place up in the rafters and sat there, all by myself, watching Angela get her degree. It was hard, but what the hell was I going to do? I wasn't going to miss Angela graduating, that's for sure. I remember watching her family all around her, supporting her, and here I was up in the rafters. It was tough on me. Very tough.

Here's how Angela saw the situation (yes, I do, on occasion, let someone else do the talking. Not often, but sometimes. Usually, so I can light up a cigar):

> In the beginning, my mother didn't like Charlie at all. But that all changed at my college graduation. Charlie was there, but he wasn't sitting with the family because of their little tiff. He was up in the rafters by himself. At that point, my mom said, "For him to come and be here for you means something to me."
>
> My mom figured, if Charlie cared enough about me to sneak into my graduation ceremony like that, he couldn't be all that bad. She respected him for that.

When Angela's mother looked up and saw me sitting there, just chilling in the rafters, I could see from her expression that she regretted her attitude toward me. After the ceremony ended, I went home to my apartment on the beach at Beverly Farms. Yeah, I was only twenty years old but, man, I was living like a king. As soon as I walked in the door, the phone rang. It was Angela.

"Charlie," she said, "my mom feels terrible. She wants you to come over and celebrate with us."

"Are you kidding?" I replied. "There's no way in hell I'm coming over! Did you see me sitting up there in the rafters? I can't believe she would treat me like that. After all I've been through . . . should I bring some dip?"

We had a great time. You'd think it would be uncomfortable for me, but it wasn't. In case you haven't figured it out by now, I'm a people person. So I was there doing my thing and *trying* to forget about what happened. Hey, I'm Greek! Okay? Blame Zeus. He could never let anything go.

When the party was over, I took Angela down to the beach and, when we got there, I asked her to marry me. Yup. That's right. That night. That's when I asked her. She said yes. When we got back home and told her mother, she replied, "I invited him over for cocktails, not to propose."

That was the spring of 1991. We planned to get married in September, which gave me six months to scrounge together enough money for the wedding.

The ceremony would take place at the Marriott, in Danvers. The hotel had three banquet rooms, with two other weddings in the other two rooms. I brought my mother-in-law down there with Angela so we could go over the details. When we got there, we found out that one of the other wedding parties wanted the room I had chosen, because they had too many guests for the one they were in.

I saw this as the perfect opportunity to get something for nothing. I turned to Angela and my mother-in-law.

"We're in a prize fight," I said. "It's the tenth round. I got him

Rick Latini, me, Bobby Latini, David Moore, and Chris Moore
at my wedding (September 1, 1991).

up against the ropes. Pretend we're having a big fight. Throw up your arms and start yelling at me. You can even swear if you want to. Just make it look like you hate my guts."

We put on quite a show, and then I went over to the manager.

"Jeez, this is horrible," I said. "We really had our eyes set on that middle hall. I'm afraid this might be a deal killer. I'm doing my best over there, but to tell you the truth, bro, they didn't like this place much to begin with. And they're going to really hate you for this. But I'll go over there and see what I can do."

After "arguing" with Angela and her mother some more, I went back to the manager and said, "Listen, I tried my best, but as you can see they're not very happy. The only thing I can think of, I guess, would be to have the wedding at the golf club at no additional charge . . ."

And that's exactly what they did.

My mother-in-law was upset because the staff became so scared of her—which had been exactly what I'd wanted. But, understand, she is anything but scary. Angela's entire family is completely different from mine. I used to call my mother-in-law Carol Brady after the irrepressibly gracious matron of *The Brady Bunch*.

My family was more like the Bundy family from *Married . . . with Children*. My brother and I would fight over the last piece of chicken. Literally, a fistfight. And Mom would get a wooden spoon and start smacking our heads. Everything was a confrontation in the Moore household. My brother would get off the couch to call his girlfriend or to get a bowl of cereal, and he'd say, "I'm savin' the whole couch." As soon as he walked away, I'd stretch right out.

When he returned, he'd demand his seat back.

"Go f—— yourself," I'd say. "It's my friggin' seat now."

Then there'd be a big blowout.

Another typical night in the Moore household involved one of our traditional seafood dinners. My brother Danny, who's a lawyer now, was always a genius. He graduated at the top of his class. But, in some ways, he's dumb as a rock, if you know what I mean.

It came down to the last littleneck clam. There it was, sitting all alone on the plate. Not a word was said. We all looked around at each other. And then back at the clam. It was just like a Clint Eastwood western. You could almost hear the theme from *The Good, the Bad, and the Ugly*. Each of us wondered who would make the first move for that clam.

It was Danny. But just as he reached in, Chris grabbed his hand. The clam went sailing up into the air and seemed to hang there for a moment. In slow motion, it started to fall. We watched it sail to the ground. Thwunk! It hit the floor and, as soon as it did, our dog Chopper went for it. But before he could get it, Danny took a nosedive off his seat, grabbed the clam, and threw it in his mouth.

That, my friends, summarizes the Moore family. Perfectly. We are not too classy to fight over the last clam.

Anyway, I was in complete culture shock for years after I met Angela and her family. I'm still trying to get over it.

Thanks for Giving Me Your Daughter . . . Now I Just Need a Place to Live

I turned twenty-one a few months after our wedding. Angela was pregnant with our son Anthony. At that point, I decided it would be a good move, politically, to get to know my in-laws better and to put the past behind us. Way behind us. What better way to do that than to live together?

I know what you're thinking: Charlie, bro, less than a year ago they wouldn't even let you in the house, and now you want to live with them? Are you crazy?

Crazy like a fox.

First of all, I figured we were so young that it would be the best thing for Angela and for her mother to get to know me better. What better way to know someone than to live under the same roof? And, of course, we'd have our own personal babysitter that we wouldn't have to pay.

Angela's parents lived in a nice, two-family, three-story house in a modest neighborhood in Beverly, Massachusetts, a few blocks up from the ocean. Downstairs, where we would live, there were three small bedrooms, a kitchen, a living room, and a dining room. Very comfortable and cozy.

On the other hand, it was an older house. You couldn't play jacks on the kitchen floor because the ball would roll down twenty feet. Fortunately, my father-in-law was a step up from Tim Allen. He could fix *anything* with a screwdriver and enough duct tape. Me? I supplied as much duct tape as necessary. That was about as much as I could manage.

My mother-in-law is phenomenal with money. She puts away a peanut here and a peanut there and next thing you know she has a peanut farm. Me, I'd eat the peanuts as soon as I cracked open the shell. Or maybe try to sell them for twice what I paid. The fact that Angela's parents weren't constantly concerned about bigger and better really impressed me.

In my family's house, it was the complete opposite. It was always, "We got a new Cadillac, and in two years, we'll get the newer Cadillac, and then a couple years later, the newest Cadillac." My dad would walk around saying, "I'm going to put a pool there, and then when I get done with the pool, I'm going to put in a tennis court."

"Do you play tennis, Dad?"

"Hell, no. But I'm going to put in a tennis court anyway, because I want a tennis court. And, if I keep it up, I might even put in a racquetball court."

He didn't play racquetball either.

My family was always about moving up to the next level. (More evidence for the What-Makes-Charlie-Moore-Run file.) So I was blown away by how content my father-in-law was. Not to mention the fact that Angela's whole family had a great relationship.

They loved each other. Sure, I had a lot of love, but the Moores expressed it in a very different way. Neither way is wrong. It's just what I was used to.

Early on, the adjustment to living together in one house was tough, even though Angela's parents were cool, down-to-earth people. But, looking back, I feel that some of my best years were spent there. It was a phenomenal time. Angela thought so, too:

> I loved living at home. I went to a local college. Once Anthony came, I didn't want to leave. I'd been living there since I was two years old, and I didn't have any problem staying put. Luckily, my parents never stepped on our toes. They never came down and bothered us. They never said, "Oh, I hear you guys bickering, you shouldn't do that." They left us alone, let us be a couple, and let us raise our own kids. At the beginning, I though we might find ourselves with that in-law syndrome, but they were awesome. And they would always invite us up for dinner. If it weren't for them, I don't know if we'd be where we are today.

My Meeting with "the Don"—I Mean, Dan

Meanwhile, I was running my father's business . . . into the ground. Chris came back from college and started to work at the store, too. In the meantime, I had another child, Nikolas. So, now you've got my brother, myself, and my father running one business. Try making that work.

One day my father brought me in and sat me down—Chris was there, too.

"Charlie," he said, "this store isn't big enough for the three of us."

I was in shock. I grew up running this business and thinking it would be mine. You could interpret it any way you wanted, you could say it nice, you could say it with a rose or a whole FTD bouquet, but the bottom line was, I was out the door.

What made it worse was that Chris was staying. It didn't seem fair. I had a family with two kids to support. Chris had no kids at the time. Chris had an MBA. The only degree I had was from the school of life, selling myself to people. In my mind, it would have been a lot easier for Chris to get a good job than it would have been for me. But he was staying and I was history. Yeah, that made it tougher.

At the time I wasn't much for reasoning, but looking back I think my dad really believed I was meant for better things and he knew I would only flourish outside of that store. And he probably figured that, the way the store was going, there was no way it could support me, Angela, and two kids (with another on the way).

So it was time to go. Adios. But before I left my dad gave me some money to get me headed in the right direction. This money was all I had to invest in the future. So my next decision . . . well, I knew it had better be a good one.

What was I going to do now? Selling cigars didn't hold much of a future for me, so my father's not-so-gentle push into the cold, cruel world should have opened up a whole bunch of opportunities for me. The trouble was, I had no other real career path in front of me. I knew I wanted to do my own thing. I just didn't know exactly what my "thing" was.

I felt frustrated. I felt angry. And I had a wife and two children to support. At one point, things got so bad I called up my old friend, Larry Saggese, late one night, and I started to get very emotional. I felt like I was left out in the dark, which I was, because not only did I get bumped from the store, but I was given virtually no guidance as to what I should do next.

In my father's defense, the store probably wouldn't have lasted if I'd stayed on. There was no way it could support three families. Times had changed. Cigarettes weren't selling like they did in 1974, when we were moving two hundred cartons a day, and you could never make much money selling lottery tickets. I felt mis-treated at the time, but now that I have some perspective, I'm okay with it. And, let's face it, if my father hadn't done what he did, would I be where I am today?

You don't have to answer. That's what they call a rhetorical question.

So there I was, with a whole lot of years in front of me, but very little idea of what to do with them. I didn't have any formal training—have I mentioned the fact that I'd failed miserably at getting a little thing called a college degree? Which meant that the only diploma on my wall was signed by my high school prin-cipal. And yeah, and there was one other little detail—and this is the last one, I promise. Money. I didn't have any. In fact, not only didn't I have any, but I owed a lot of what I didn't have to, oh, what are those people called? Oh, yeah, credit card companies.

I had to move on. But where was I going? How was I going to get there? In short, what did I want to do with the rest of my life? I decided to take the scientific route and make an inventory of what I knew, what I did best, and what I liked. Believe me, the list wasn't all that long.

1. I knew how to sell things. Cigars. Lottery tickets. Comic books. Cars. Myself.
2. I liked to fish.
3. I liked to make people laugh.

Dan Moore, the Field General, might as well get a word in here:

Charlie was born on a Saturday at approximately two o'clock in the afternoon. We had three boys and didn't know whether to expect a girl or another boy. I was home taking care of the kids when I got a call from the hospital, just about kick-off time, say-ing I'd had another boy. I lay down on the bed and couldn't stop laughing. Oh, my God, I thought. Four boys in a row. I laughed and laughed and maybe that's why Charlie's always been such a laughing kind of guy.

It was my turn to choose, so I named him after a great-uncle of mine that I'd always liked. I gave him Joseph as a middle name after the doctor who called me from the delivery room, who happened to be a good friend of mine. Charles Joseph Moore, but I used to call him Charlie Joe. I was the only one who did that, though.

Charlie was different from the other boys. He was always a self-starter. Never had to worry about him. If he wanted to do something he would go out and learn how to do it on his own. Take ice skating, for example. All the boys were ice skaters but one day I look outside and there's Charlie, four or five years old, tying on a pair of his brother's skates, which were much too big for him. He's goes out there by himself trying to learn how to ice skate. The next thing I know, he's doing it.

Charlie was always very close with his sister, who came two years after him. They used to play together and organize all kinds of events. They had their own little band. They'd play records and he would sing or he would play the drums while she sang. He was actually pretty good. Charlie was always the showman. He was always on stage.

I used to take Charlie out fishing with me. We had a good-sized boat that I kept at Boston Harbor, and we'd take the kids down there on weekends. I had fishing rods and reels for all of them, but the only one who ever used them was Charlie. He was the guy who liked to fish. He'd be out there fishing all the time, or he'd be swimming, which he loved to do. He just loved jumping in the water and splashing around. He was a real water baby.

When you have children, you'll often hear a knock on the door and when you go to answer it there's a bunch of kids there and they say, "Can so-and-so come out and play?" With Charlie, there'd be a bunch of men standing around the marina and

My sister Juliana and me when we were little kids.

they'd come up to me and say, "Can Charlie come out and fish?" At the time, Charlie was only about seven or eight years old!

Around ten o'clock at night, Charlie's mother would call me on the boat and ask, "Is Charlie okay?"

"He's fine," I'd say.

"Is he sleeping?"

"Let me check." I'd take a look, come back, and pick up the phone. "Yeah, he's sleeping." But he was actually fishing for smelt with the guys. He just loved to fish, and he was very good at it.

One day, my friend Norman asked me to go fishing with him. I took Charlie, who was about nine at the time, and Julie, who was seven. We all went fishing off Plymouth. I've had kids on boats before and they invariably get their lines tangled up and it's an unbearable mess trying to untangle them. So I said to Julie, "You stay over on that side and do your fishing over there, and Charlie, you stay over on this side and you do your fishing here."

Meanwhile, I was talking to Norman and his girlfriend and, suddenly, I look over and Charlie and Julie are on the same side of the boat and having big trouble.

"I thought I told you guys to stay separate."

"There's something wrong with the line," Charlie said. So I grab one line and it was heavy. Then I grab the other line and it was heavy, too. I pull both lines up and there are two ten-pound cods on one line, and another ten-pound cod on the other line. They caught thirty pounds of cod in no time flat. That was a great day. We caught so damn many cod I didn't know what to do with them.

Eventually, I gave Charlie a boat of his own—a Boston Whaler. His mother was very concerned about it—he was only a child—so to appease her I had a smaller, twenty-horsepower engine installed. Charlie went all over Boston Harbor in that thing.

Charlie had a lot of friends, but none of them had the interest in fishing that he had. Charlie was the fisherman, and I don't know where he got that from because I wasn't a great fisherman either, though my father was.

Charlie was also very active in sports. He was a very good athlete, and particularly good at baseball. He was a terrific pitcher and it was amazing what he could do with that ball. He played football, too—if he didn't, I probably would have thrown him out of the house.

Charlie wasn't a great student. He wasn't disobedient, but the problem with him was he couldn't stop talking. That was his nature. He could talk the legs off a chair.

Charlie was able to put those two qualities together—talking and fishing—and found a way to make it work for him.

My father was the one who introduced me to saltwater fishing, but it was my father-in-law, Dick, who got me into freshwater fishing. Angela and I would go out with him and I'd sit there on the lake, smoking a cigar and casting a line. At first,

I didn't know what the hell I was doing, but since I'm pretty athletic it wasn't long before I got a clue. And when I did, I began to like it.

It's True: There Is No Off Position on the Genius Switch

So, what was I going to do with myself? Let's check back to that list, specifically items #1 and #2.

Sales. Fishing. Fishing. Sales. Even without a college education, I knew that my skill at fishing combined with my natural salesmanship made opening a tackle store a natural decision. It made perfect sense . . . at the time.

Of course, you need money to open a store and I didn't have anything but the money my dad gave me, which we were using to live on. But I did have a credit card—they mail those things to anyone with an address—so, to start the ball rolling, I bought a 170-Nitro fishing boat.

Then it was time for Step 2: actually opening up that tackle store. On credit, of course. Thank you very much, Visa and MasterCard. I called it Bass Country, and it was on Cabot Street in Beverly, Massachusetts.

I was pretty excited about it—for the first time in my life, I had a store that wasn't within another store. But it didn't take long for things to go sour.

I opened Bass Country in the late fall, in the dead of what was a particularly bleak New England winter, which, looking back on it, wasn't the ideal time to start a business dedicated to the celebration of the great outdoors.

In the beginning, because we were the new store on the block, people were curious and came in to look around. They weren't actually buying anything, but at least there was the illusion of something going on. But once winter settled in, nothing. I mean, *nothing*. No one came into the store—why should they? I spent most of the time dreaming about a sudden run on fishing equipment, despite the remote chances of ice fishing going mainstream in my neck of the woods. Although that's not to say that there weren't a few ice fisherman who showed up wanting to buy my shiners.

Most of the day, I sat around with nothing to do and no one to talk to. So, partly to pass the time and partly to motivate anyone who might wander in to actually buy something, I brought a TV down to the store and tuned it to outdoor shows. A great idea, right? Someone walks in, sees someone fishing on screen, says to themselves, "You know, come to think of it, I could use a couple of lures." Only problem was, there was no one there for it to motivate except me. And for some reason it had the opposite effect: I just got depressed because (a) it reminded me of the business I wasn't doing, and (b) the shows sucked.

Since I wasn't doing any business, I thought I might as well make myself useful by giving Angela a much needed break. So, I brought the kids and their toys down to the store, which quickly turned Bass

Anthony and Nikolas making a chocolate something-or-other.
Oh yeah, a mess.

Country into Mad Fisherman Daycare. Though I seriously doubt that most daycare centers have fishing hooks hanging from the wall.

My kids, Anthony and Nikolas, were having a great time watching the movie *The Little Rascals* and running around with their toys, riding their bikes and stuff, which wasn't really a problem, since there was little chance of hitting anyone except me, while I contemplated whether I should hang myself with fishing line or jump off a bridge.

It didn't seem like things could get any worse, but they did. First, Angela's brother Rick got an infection in his lungs, which was a total surprise for someone as young, healthy, and full of life as he was. He was really sick and it was touch and go there for a while.

So let's take stock: no money, one beat-up truck, I'm selling maybe three shiners a day, and now Angela is dealing with her sick brother. Pretty grim, huh? But wait, it gets worse.

About a week and a half later, Chris, his wife Colleen, Angela, and I are called in to have a sit-down with my mom and dad. They told us that my brother Dave, with whom I'm the closest—we're like two peas in a pod—was extremely sick. Once the shock wore off—but, trust me, it never wears completely off—we knew that someone needed to go out to California to be with him and to figure out exactly what the situation was. Chris and my brother, Danny, and I decided to go.

Immediately, my father-in-law, Dickie, and his brother, Bob Latini, and my brother-in-law, Bobby Latini, who was seventeen, offered to run the store while I was away. Of course, there was nothing much going on there anyway, but that wasn't the point. The offer was incredible. And even more incredible was that Colleen had a bunch of frequent-flyer miles and offered to pay for my ticket, which I wouldn't have been able to pay for myself.

So, Chris and Danny and I get on the plane—I'm laughing and joking, trying to keep the situation light—and Chris turns to me and says, "Hey, bro, how much money did you bring with you for the trip?"

"Forty dollars."

"Forty dollars!"

"Yeah, forty dollars. That's all I've got to my name."

So, Chris wound up paying for the whole trip.

When we landed, I found a phone and called Angela, just to let her know that we'd landed safely. It turned out to be a more important call than that, because that's when she told me we were having a baby girl.

As it turned out, both Rick and Dave made great recoveries, Dave against all odds. And what that proved to me is that there must be a strong determination gene in the Moore family.

By the time I got back from California, the handwriting was on the wall. And what it said was: "It's over." The time I spent with Dave kind of opened my eyes to the fact that you don't have much time on this earth, so you'd better use it well.

Get the picture? It was bad. Real bad. And being back at the store didn't help. I remember people coming into the store while I was in the back changing diapers. "Hey, can I get a couple of shiners?"

"Yeah, sure. I'll be right with you after I finish with the Pampers."

Basically, the store had become a great place for me to go and lose money. Money I didn't even have, by the way. The only ones who actually came in, besides my kids, were a few friends of mine, and they sure as hell didn't buy anything. Customers would buy a reel, then they'd come back to friggin' exchange it, and all I'm making is five bucks. In that first month, I realized that I'd be sitting there nickel-and-diming myself for the next thirty years. That's not what I had in mind when I made that list.

But something good did come out of those tough times: I discovered the loyalty of my in-laws. They were the ones who came in and worked that store, even helping to build the walls. My mother-in-law gave me money; my father-in-law gave me time—and his tools—but I did hold up my end by supplying the duct tape.

I put in this big lure order for crank baits, which was the stupidest thing I ever did. Suddenly, I owed $565 for crank baits.

And those damn crank baits sat on the wall for weeks. Not one person bought one. Every time my mother-in-law came into the store, I'd see her glance over at those crank baits—because she'd had to pay for them; otherwise, I couldn't have afforded them. After a couple weeks of those crank baits just sitting there, before my mother-in-law would come in, I'd run over and take four or five off of them off the rack and stash them in a drawer, just to give the illusion that someone was buying them. As soon as she'd leave, I'd put them back up on the wall.

After a month or two, pretty much everybody realized that it wasn't going to happen for me. Even now, it's very emotional for me to talk about those times, the times when I was really down on my luck. My father-in-law, Dickie, would work the store to give me a break, which meant a lot to me. I'd come in after he'd worked for three or four hours and he would say, "We sold some cigars and a couple of lures and some spare baits. We made $42.50."

"That's great," I'd say.

After a couple of days of us doing well, or rather Dickie doing well, I happened to be upstairs in his bedroom. I opened up this bag and found all the "sold" lures and cigars. I just started to cry. I never told Dickie about that because, quite frankly, I needed the $42.50.

"It's Always Darkest Before the Dawn" . . . What a Load of Crap *That* Is

If I thought things couldn't get any worse, I was wrong. One day, I was sitting there alone, of course, except for Anthony and Nikolas. While they were playing in the background, I was contemplating suicide. Yes, it was that grim. If somebody came in at that moment to rob me, I would have said, "Shoot me before you leave and why don't you take the crank baits with you, because it'll help my mother-in-law. Just take the crank baits and shoot me!"

While I'm in the midst of all these exit strategies, the door opens and in walks this guy dressed in a suit and tie. Not my typical customer profile.

"How ya doin'?" he says.

"I'm doin' fine," I say, lying through my teeth.

"I work for the mayor's office. What's your name?"

"Charlie Moore."

"Well, Mr. Moore, we've got a problem."

Now I've got lots of problems, most of which I know all too well, so I don't need this guy to list them for me. Nor do I need him to give me any new ones, although I have a sneaking suspicion that that's exactly what's going to happen.

"Oh yeah, what's that?"

"Well, I see that you've got a truck parked in front of your store and in the back of that truck there's a sign that says CIGARS. First of all, the truck is parked illegally, so you've got to get it out of there, and second of all, you can't keep that sign there."

Now remember, I'm on death's door. I got no money. I can't pay for anything. In fact, things had gotten so bad that I'd started selling individual cigars to bring in some cash, which explains the sign. And, to be quite honest, the cigars were the only thing that was keeping the door open. And now this guy, from the mayor's office, no less, is coming into my store telling me I've got to take down my sign.

Did he just happen to be passing by, see the truck and the sign, and think, "Well, what we've got here is a violation of City Code 273?" Nope. I'm pretty sure the city was called by the liquor store owner next door. That guy was always busting my chops because he didn't want my truck parked there, either because he thought it was an eyesore or because he wanted the spot for himself.

Talk about kicking a dog when he's down. Here's this guy, one of the mayor's henchmen, coming in to bully just because the guy next door was complaining. Of course, later, the guy in the liquor store acted as if he had no idea what I was talking about.

They say shit always runs downhill and, unfortunately for me,

I was at the bottom of that hill. What would I do? True, I could beat the crap out of the liquor store owner. Or I could hire a lawyer with the money from all those crank baits I was selling. Or maybe I could bribe the guy from the mayor's office with two or three crank baits to leave me alone. Or I could just move my truck and take the sign down.

No truck parked in front of the store, no sign on the street, no cigar sales, equaled total disaster, making it impossible to stay in business.

The Cigar Sign That Broke the Camel's Back

To make matters even worse, in the middle of this argument between me and the guy from the mayor's office, Nikolas started crying. He needed to have his diaper changed. Only there were no more diapers. Meanwhile, Anthony says to me, "Dad, I'm hungry."

But I got no food. And I got no diapers. All I got is cigars, lures, and bait. So, I put Nikolas in the carriage and I say to Anthony, "Let's go home."

On my way out, I grabbed a cigar and locked the door behind me. Frankly, I don't remember much of that afternoon, because it felt like I was walking down the center of Cabot Street, waiting for a bus to hit me. I moved through a cloud of anger, contemplating what to do with my life from that point forward. The truth of the matter is, I don't remember everything that happened on that walk, but I do remember the mind-set. That I remember well.

I'm walking home with my two kids, smoking a mild, five-dollar Macanudo cigar. It felt like it took five years to get home, but during those five years I do remember taking a deep puff on that Macanudo, letting the smoke out slowly, and saying to myself, "What the hell am I gonna do with the rest of my life? I have no college degree. I have no money. I have no food. I have no diapers. I have no cigar sign. But I do have plenty of crank baits, which nobody wants."

What the hell do I do?

When the Going Gets Tough, the Tough Go on Vacation

When we hit rock bottom it was *rock* bottom. Again, we didn't even have enough money to buy food for our kids. We couldn't buy diapers. It was that bad. I don't know if anyone in my family realized how bad it really was.

During that period, my in-laws would rent a cabin in Maine for the month of July. We didn't have enough money to rent our own cabin so sometimes we would stay with them. It got pretty tight in there, what with Angela, Anthony, Nikolas, and me, but we were outdoors most of the time, so it didn't really matter much.

Angela's sister, Christine, and her husband, Bill, and their family had their own cabin. Bill was doing pretty well at the time. He wasn't exactly lighting the world on fire, but to us his family seemed like the Rockefellers because they could do things that we couldn't. There was never any bitterness, but I have to admit that sometimes I thought, "It'd be nice to go to the grocery store and be able to get food." Or, "It'd be nice to have a vehicle that worked."

Maine offered phenomenal fishing. One day, about halfway into their vacation, my father-in-law called me and said, "The fish are biting, Charlie. Oh, my God, while I'm standing here talking to you I just caught a smallmouth."

"I'm coming up, Dickie. I swear to God I'm coming up."

When my father-in-law told me he'd caught that fish, my whole life changed. I hung up the phone, turned to Angela, and said, "Pack up the kids. We're going up to Maine to visit your parents. We're going on this camping trip if it kills us. Let's drag out the friggin' pickup truck. Daddy needs a vacation."

I had this big, green, four-speed F-250, a true redneck truck with raised tires and featuring an eight-foot bed. It was the only vehicle we had and it wasn't worth any money, other than the tires and rims, maybe. It wasn't anything to write home about, but I loved it. I put Nikolas in his car seat in the middle, and Angela sat on the outside with Anthony on her lap (Angela was almost nine months pregnant at this point with our third child, Kaitlin), and we were off.

Talk about a redneck vacation—it was totally "blue light special," baby, because we were going *camping*. Sure, I've got the beat-up truck, but I've got no money. In fact, I'm counting change for gas.

We drove that son-of-a-gun all the way up to Maine. That thing was hitting every bump. I was listening to Alan Jackson on the tape player, my window was down, I was smoking a cigar, and the kids were all packed in the front with us. I looked over at Angela. She was a real trooper, man. She was so happy we were going and, even though she was worried about having the baby, she was still thrilled to go up there and spend time with her parents.

That was a great time and, to me, that is the definition of true love, right there. And the meaning of success. Because when you're up against the wall and you can still crack a smile and feel good about yourself, that's it. Most people can't feel good because they're not driving what they want. But although I didn't have the things that I wanted, I had my family, which is more important to me than anything, and we were going fishing. To me, that is the distinction between fishermen like myself and guys who, in a similar situation, would call it a day, sit back on the couch, and watch TV.

Yes, Mr. Coppola, I'm Ready for My Close-Up

Once I got back to the real world, I had to deal with my real life. And what I was going to do with it.

As a kid, I had always wanted to be the starting quarterback for the Washington Redskins or the centerfielder for the Boston Red Sox and be, you know, famous. Well, the QB and centerfield things weren't looking too good, so that left just the "famous" thing, which really appealed to me since I had always craved attention, even as a kid. Big surprise, huh?

At that point, I knew the outdoor store was pretty much over, but one good thing about the experience was the TV on the counter which, when it wasn't tuned to *The Little Rascals* for my kids, would run those outdoor fishing shows that taped throughout the country.

People—notice, I didn't say customers—would come in and ask me, "Don't you get bored?" and I'd say, "Yeah, but I keep myself as busy as I can." Then they'd reply, "No. I mean watching these shows."

Hell, yeah, I got bored. Why wouldn't I? Most of them were pretty damn bad. And that's why, after a while, I said to myself, "I can do better."

So, that day, while walking with my two kids, smoking that five-dollar cigar, and trying to figure out the meaning of life, *my life,* it hit me, right between Appleton Avenue and Prospect Street.

"Ya know what?" I thought. "I'm gonna get my own TV show. No, really. I am."

Would You Like Fries with That Coke?

Becoming a TV star wasn't quite as far-fetched as it seemed. Okay, maybe it was. But it didn't feel that way to me.

It wasn't as if I hadn't thought about it before. When I was in the store with the TV on, people would come in and shoot the breeze with me—hey, they certainly weren't there to buy anything. They knew I liked to fish and they knew I had a good personality, so they started saying things like, "Hey, Charlie, you should get your own show." It sounded like a fine idea to me so, while the store was still open, I went home and actually wrote a treatment for my first TV show. I called it *Charlie Moore Outdoors*. What I was aiming for was "fine comedy entertainment." That was the recipe for the show. Pure and simple. Show 'em how to fish. Make 'em laugh. Repeat.

But let's back it up again to that fateful day when I left the store with my two kids. I remember getting home, closing the door, and having a complete emotional meltdown. I broke things—plates, cups, anything that was handy—while my kids sat there, watching me. I had no idea what to do. I had no money, no food, and all the bills were due. And now the mayor of Beverly wanted me to take my sign down. But before it got really ugly, I picked up the phone and called Angela who, by the way, was out trying to get another job because the part-time job she had at a law firm wasn't bringing in enough money. I told her to drop what she was doing and come home. And when she got there, I was lying on the kitchen floor, pretty close to tears.

"I really don't want to do this anymore. I don't think this is what I should be doing."

It was at this point that Angela realized just how desperate things were. It felt like I was on *Survivor* and I was the one voted off the island and, unfortunately, they didn't tell me where to go or what to do. Hey, where's the manual for what happens when you get voted off the island? I felt so alone. The future couldn't have looked any bleaker.

People can starve for a week and, when they eat, they're fine, but to be desperate and on thin ice for a long period of time is the real test of human spirit. I was at the breaking point and I needed to make a decision as to what we were going to do, because what I was doing just wasn't cutting it. I wasn't going to spend the rest of my life sitting around selling stuff and having the mayor shake me down like crap for a sign in front of my store.

But now, at least, I had an answer. I was going to be a TV star! That would solve everything. Not only would I have more than enough money to put food on the table, but I'd also be famous!

But first, before I embarked on my new career in television, I had to close Bass Country. So, I picked myself up off the floor and said, "We're going to close the store right now." Just like that.

I called my father-in-law, who at the time worked for Sylvania.

"Hey, Dickie, can you get me like, oh, I don't know, forty-two empty boxes, so we can fill them up with crap I never sold?"

Once provided with plenty of boxes, Angela and I rallied the troops. We brought boxes over and loaded them up and, by the end of the day, Bass Country was nothing more than a not-so-fond memory.

After it was all over, I remember standing there looking at all those boxes.

"Man, I've got like a ton of lures," I pointed out to Dickie. "So, filming all those shows, I'll have no problem with outdoor tackle and gear. Just don't mention any of this to the credit card companies I owe money to."

And you know what? After we closed up shop no one missed us, or even noticed we weren't open anymore. Except maybe some of my friends, who didn't have a place to hang out and watch fishing shows anymore.

Here's how Angela saw things:

> Charlie is crazy. I know it and he knows it. In the beginning, when he had this idea for a fishing show, I was very supportive of him. But it was difficult because of where we were financially—we already had two kids and I was pregnant with Kaitlin. For him to say, "Hey, I'm taking all of our savings"—which wasn't much, by the way—"to buy a boat so we can get this thing started," was very difficult.
>
> But it was Charlie's passion and I always knew he had talent. He's also very stubborn. He knows he's going to get his way. So I think his attitude made me believe in him, even if no one else did. I know that when he wants something, he'll get it, no matter what it is. So, I was one hundred percent supportive of him, even though I know there were people back then who said we shouldn't have done what we did because of our situation. But I wasn't one of those wives who says, "Well, we have to be practical. We don't have money and we've got another child on the way . . ." My feeling was, "This is where your heart is? Go for it."

Now that the store was officially closed—some might say that it never truly opened—the search for my career in television began. Man, I gotta tell ya, I went through the Yellow Pages and the

Help Wanted sections of every newspaper and, for the life of me, I could not find one single listing for a job to be a Famous TV Host. What a blow. So it was on to Plan B.

Déjà Vu All Over Again

Meanwhile, I had no job and no money and, when I looked around, I saw that I still had a family to feed. Oh, and I also had that boat . . . which still wasn't paid for, by the way. I tried to get a job, but I couldn't find one. Finally, I stumbled across a Texaco station near the highway that was looking for help. I figured I could pump gas until I got that TV gig.

The owner turned me down.

As a last resort, I called my old friend, Larry Saggese, owner of Saggese Landscaping in Danvers, Massachusetts. I told Larry what was going on in my life, explaining my entire situation. I told him I really needed a favor and Larry came through for me. He gave me a job. Did I know anything about landscaping? Sure: you were supposed to make the landscape look good.

How to go about doing that, I had no clue.

I spent most of the day blowing leaves around—I actually got pretty good at that, as a matter of fact. I was taking home *maybe* a couple hundred bucks a week. After we paid our bills, the ones that absolutely had to be paid, Angela and I were living on something like seventy dollars a week, which was supposed to pay for groceries for us and the three kids. We couldn't afford diapers. We couldn't afford formula. And my mother-in-law let the rent slide.

Meanwhile, I was still beating the bushes, so to speak, to get my real career on track. One of the lawns I worked on belonged to Billy Costa, a host on the local cable network and a big radio DJ on KISS 108. One day, I pitched him the idea for my show. He was like, "Alright kid, get back to mowing and blowing." Can you blame him? After all, I was his landscaper. And by the way, in case you haven't picked this up by now, I sucked at landscaping!

I Hear Ya Knockin', But You Can't Come In

Here in New England, local sports are featured on the New England Sports Network, NESN, which is owned by the Boston Red Sox and Boston Bruins. I figured, hey, if I'm gonna make a run at this, this is where I have to start. So, I called NESN—they're in the phone book, you know—and I left them all kinds of creative messages. I was having conversations with the answering machine like it was a secretary. In fact, that machine and I became best friend. But for some unknown reason, no one from NESN ever called me back. Imagine that.

At the same time, I contacted a friend of mine named Johnny Cacciatore, who knew John Slattery, who worked for NESN. I went to Johnny with the outline for the show I'd created, and he helped me fine-tune it and then presented it to Slattery.

After a few weeks, I finally managed to get a hold of Bob Whitelaw, who was the vice president in charge of programming at NESN. Bob explained to me that they were not interested in having me on their network.

"Come on, man," I said. "There's no way I'm taking no for an answer." I figured I was doing them a favor, giving them the opportunity to air my show. But they didn't see it that way. I begged and pleaded and begged some more.

"Okay," Bob relented. "Why don't you come down to Fenway Park"—that's where their office was located—"and I'll tell you no to your face."

At first I thought, I can't believe what a jerk this guy is. But then I realized: No. Wait. This is . . . a meeting! Yes! Charlie Moore is taking a meeting with the suits at NESN!

I was on my way.

Hi, My Name's Charlie Moore and I'm Going to Be NESN's Next Big TV Star

I went down there and met with Bob Whitelaw and another guy named Peter Frechette. I walked in with a couple of fishing poles and a photo album filled with pictures of me and fish and, to be honest, some of the fish weren't even mine.

I walked around the table to where Whitelaw and Frechette sat and said, "Hey, let me show you my resume."

I opened up the album to photographs of me holding up a bunch of fish. It was hilarious. At least I thought so. But for some reason, they didn't seem all that impressed and, when I started to walk out of the room, I heard Whitelaw say, "Give him a couple days, and he's gone."

At first, Bob wouldn't give me an inch. From the time I left that office, I was constantly on the phone, putting the bug in their ear. Finally, one day Frechette let it slip that they were doing a new show called *Front Row,* which was a sports magazine show, three or four different segments per half hour. As soon as I heard that, I smelled an opportunity. Rather than have them front me for a whole half-hour show, I thought, maybe they'd let me do a segment on *Front Row.*

"Hey," I said to myself, "if I can get three or four minutes, that'd be a start." So, when I finally got Frechette on the phone again, I brought up *Front Row.*

"How about doing something a little weird, a little off-center. Stories that don't have to do with major sports or high school girls playing lacrosse. How about doing stories on fishing? How about we just go shoot some fishing stuff with regular guys, like me?"

Finally, after a lot more agitating on my side, they agreed to take a few shows from me. Now, to be perfectly honest, I had absolutely no inkling that there was anybody out there who wanted to watch fishing, especially *me* fishing, but what the heck? I had my foot in the door. I was on my way. The rest, I thought, would be a piece of cake.

As it turned out, it wasn't anywhere near that easy, in large part because I didn't know what the hell was going on or what I was actually going to do.

But that wasn't going to stop me.

Okay, the Camera's Rolling. Now What?

Now that I had the green light from NESN, it was time for me to put up or shut up.

They had given me a five-minute segment—*on TV!*—but I had absolutely no idea what I was going to do with it. Sure, I was excited about the opportunity, but I felt I'd pushed them so much, it was like begging a girl to go out with you and she finally says yes just to shut you up:

"Okay, fine, but only for one date . . . and we're gonna go to lunch, not dinner. And I've only got forty-five minutes for lunch . . . and we gotta get a seat right near the door, so I can get out of there quick, if I have to."

After the initial excitement, it occurred to me that I had pushed so hard only to get a few shows for fifty bucks an episode. And it wasn't even my own show.

They assigned a guy named Bob Sylvester to be my producer. Bob is a New Englander. He grew up in Auburn, Maine. Coincidentally, he married his wife Carolyn in September 1991, the same week Angela and I got married. He'd started as an intern at NESN in January 1992, and worked his way up from master control, to game edit for the Red Sox and the Bruins, to audio and stats for the Bruins and the Sox, and to general production assistant. It took him eighteen months of working overnight master control at NESN before he could finally get hired full-time.

When I spoke to Bob on the phone, he told me he was a saltwater fishing guy and didn't know anything about freshwater fishing. I told him I'd change all that, starting with when I'd meet him up at Lake Chebacco, in Hamilton, Massachusetts, where I'd fished with my father-in-law and brother-in-law many times.

And so for this, the very first *Front Row* show, I drove up to Lake Chebbaco, dragging along the boat I hadn't paid for yet. I got there early but I decided not to launch until Bob and the cameraman, Mike Cole, got there. It just so happened that, in Boston that morning, a tractor-trailer had jackknifed under a bridge. Traffic out of the city was backed up for hours, which meant that Bob and Mike were delayed. But I didn't know that. Remember, this was 1996, before everyone had cell phones.

So, I'm standing there, looking at my watch every three seconds, wondering where the hell they were. After a while, I began to think that maybe the suits at NESN had held a meeting that morning: "Hey," they'd said. "Wouldn't it be funny if we left that kid up there all day waiting for the camera crew to arrive? That'd finally get him off our backs, wouldn't it?"

So that was it, I thought. They weren't coming. Before the first show had even happened, I'm standing there with a rod in one hand and my lures in the other, with the crickets going crick, crick, crick, thinking, well, it was good while it lasted—one whole day. And, by the way, do you think I'm still going to get my fifty bucks? Because I could really use it. After all, I gave up a whole day of blowing leaves for this.

Finally, they showed up. And man, was I relieved. We introduced ourselves, went right to the ramp, and launched the boat into the water. We started singing who knows what—we were happy just to get started—and Mike started filming. Suddenly, as we're moving out onto the lake, I noticed a little problem: the boat was taking on water. In case you don't know, that's not supposed to happen. The water's supposed to stay on the outside of the boat, with the fish—until I catch them.

Being a man of action, I immediately located where the water was coming in, stuck my hand down there and realized that there was no plug where there should have been a plug. Instead of being in the boat, holding out the water, the plug was sitting back on my driveway, where I'd left it. So, like the Little Dutch Boy, I kept my hand on the hole to keep the water from coming in, and we got the boat back up on the beach. I found something to clog up the hole and then we got back out onto the water and started filming.

Once we were out there on the lake again, I must have done 27,000 takes, because I had no idea what they wanted from me. When the camera was on, I was nervous, but when the camera was turned off, I relaxed, saying things like, "Hey, that's a nice camera you got there, Mike. Sure you know how to work it?" I talked about how the camera was an aphrodisiac and how we could take it and get free meals and how women flash us.

That first segment was too straightforward, like a fastball right down the middle. It was like, "I'm Charlie Moore and this is what we're going to do today. We're going to try to catch bass. Blah, blah, blah." Bland.

But that wasn't the only problem. In fact, it probably would have been okay if I'd actually caught a single bass that day. In fact, I didn't catch anything, unless you count a couple of croppy you'd need a magnifying glass and tweezers to eat. At the end of the day, I stared right into the camera and said, in my best TV host voice, "Hey, next week we'll come back here again and actually catch a fish!" If you're keeping score, that counts as the first on-camera ad-lib I did.

I look back now and it seems funny to me, but it wasn't funny then. Not funny at all. In fact, at the time I'm thinking, "Hey, Charlie, at least you're going to make the Guinness Book of Records with the shortest TV run ever—five minutes."

Here's Bob's take on what happened:

When I first met Charlie, I remember thinking he was really young. He was so nervous that it took us several takes just to get the opening. Finally, after Charlie figured out how to keep the boat from sinking into the lake, we got out on the water. But Charlie had some trouble catching fish, which made him even more

Sal Malguarnera, NESN cameraman, and
me on Lake Winnipesaukee. I'm holding
a six-pound and a four-pound bass.

nervous. Finally, he caught a couple of croppy, which is what they call pan fish. You can eat them, but they aren't sport fish. And they were little. After about four or five hours on the water, I said, "Okay, that's it. We gotta go." And that was the end of that.

I remember, though, that after we shut the camera down Charlie was very funny. He was making jokes and having a really good time—you know, just like a regular guy. We talked about how the fishing shows that we both watched—he watched more of the freshwater ones, I watched more of the saltwater ones—were really kind of boring, clinical, and technical.

I think the whole thing caught him by surprise that he was actually getting a shot. But the thing is, he made the most of whatever he was given. He took it, maximized it, and then got some more.

Fortunately, the second time we went out there things went a little better. I went out with a guy named Carl Woughter. It was late May, early June, and at that time of year the fishing was really good. At one point Carl said, "Jesus, Charlie, you're going crazy," and Bob decided to use that line on the promo for the next show.

The show suddenly started to gel when I began to get used to my surroundings and the people I was working with. I learned what they could do, what I could do, and how I could do it. It's like with any sport. Once you're well into the season, the team, no matter how bad it was at the beginning, starts to improve. And in that second show, my personality started to come out.

Bob can attest to that:

> The second show, Charlie was looser. He started doing some of the funny stuff when the camera was on that he had been doing when it was off. He wasn't being so clinical, so technical. He wasn't talking about baits and lures. He was being funny.
>
> There was one moment that really stood out and cracked us up. We were catching smallmouth bass and Carl, who is a very old-school, heavyset guy, was sitting on a stool in front of the boat. It was a real contrast: Charlie's electric bundle of energy, and Carl, the polar opposite. Charlie caught a smallmouth bass. He hauls it out of the water and goes, "I got him. I got him!" and then the fish wiggled out of his hand and fell onto the boat and Charlie had to chase it around for five, ten seconds. Then he picked it up and said, "I lost him and now I got him again!" His delivery was very funny.
>
> Now, at that time of year the fish's eyes turn red, like they're bloodshot. Carl turns to Charlie and says, "Let's tell the people at home why their eyes turn red." And Charlie goes, "Because they were out drinking a lot of vodka last night."

At the time, I remember thinking, "What fishing shows need are more energy, more fun, and Charlie's the guy who can give that to us."

Of course, you ask Bob and he'll tell you, "I told Charlie to be funny." Yeah, right. Like he was a genius. Like he swooped in like Producerman, with a big P on his shirt. Bobby! Listen, I was that way when I was seven. My personality was my personality. You could be the greatest producer or editor in the world, but what you can't do is create a personality.

The bottom line about those first few shows is that Bob says it was this, Angela says it was that, Mike Cole says it was another thing. The reality, the truth, let it be known, was that I started to feel real comfortable with the guys out there. In the beginning, I didn't know who they were, they didn't know who I was. But hell, I was always this way. Mike was always who he is. Bob's who he is. My father is always who he is. You are who you are. You start to feel comfortable around people, you start to open up to people, and things start to gel. And that's what really happened. In the beginning, I didn't know what I could say. I worried about swearing. I worried: Can I say this? Can I say that? Are they gonna air this? Are they gonna air that?

But once I started to feel comfortable with everybody, the show started to evolve. I loosened up a little bit. I started saying things like, "Hey, man, we can't fish. Pass the beef jerky." That type of stuff. Basically, we all just started to have fun—as if we were going, well, fishing!

The Boat Gets Launched into the Water. And This Time the Plug Is In.

The progress of the show was slow. In the beginning, I was just trying to teach people how to fish and I was nervous, as dry as an overcooked potato. But once the camera was shut off, and we started talking about the stuff guys talk about when they're fishing—girls, money, rock and roll—that was the real me.

By the second or third show, we'd added two or three jokes, and then, by the fourth episode, we really started to click. You could see that something was going on. All of a sudden we had a lot of good things to build on. It was easy because I wasn't really creating something new, I was just being myself. The inner kid became the outer kid, if you know what I mean. By the fourth episode, I just started to talk, like I was doing off-camera. Being myself. In the beginning, that wasn't me on camera. It was just some guy who was trying to copy what he'd seen before. And not doing it very well, by the way. But that changed. Slowly. But it did.

There is no one show I can point to where I found my own voice. I felt my way through it and, gradually, more and more of my own personality came out. I would say something funny on camera and, in the editing room, Bob saw that the pure fishing part was slow and the Charlie Moore part wasn't. That's when the show took on a personality (mine) and life (mine) of its own. I don't mean to sound egotistical here. It's not about me, per se. It's about finding my own, unique voice and then using that voice. It's about being genuine. That wasn't a character on screen. That was me. And that's what the viewers started to respond to.

Crazy Is As Crazy Does

The first really crazy thing I did on camera was on Bear Lake in Bridgeton, Maine, during our first year on *Front Row*. The fishing was unbelievable. I'd never seen so many fish in one place in my life. But there was one damn fish that kept biting on my line, but I could not come up with him. I had him—it was a smallmouth, three pounds at least. I reeled him in from about thirty feet of water, but then I lost him. Then, I caught him again. And then I lost him again. It was like this fish was taunting me.

Finally, I gave up and fished somewhere else for the rest of the show. But I wasn't going to let a fish beat me, so just before we were ready to wrap it up for the day, I said to the guys, "Let's go back to the spot where I lost that fish and just film a couple of castoffs." So, we got there and I threw a couple casts and then I turned to the camera and said, "Let's wrap up this episode of *Front Row.* I'm Charlie Moore and we came out to Bear Lake today to have some fun and I think we did that. We were trying to catch some fish, and we did that, too. But as for that one fish that got away, the one I couldn't catch . . . ," and then, before I can finish my sentence, I feel a tug on the line. "Hold on! I got him! I got him!" I wasn't kidding around. It was the real thing. And the next thing I knew, I was reeling him in.

"Oh my God, it's a four-pound smallmouth!"

And then, just as I was reeling him in—he was practically in the boat!—he jumped off the line.

I thought, how great would it be if I just jumped into the lake for it.

So, that's what we decided to do. But we knew I only had one shot at it because I'd have to rip off my mic and jump in the lake and I didn't have another change of clothing. So, we got everything set up and then I pretended I had one on my line but lost it.

"That's it!" I screamed. "I'm not taking this anymore! I'm going after this fish. I'm going in after it."

And, completely dressed, I jumped right into the lake. As I treaded water, I looked up at the camera and said, "I'm looking for that fish but, until next week, I'm Charlie Moore, and thanks for watching." And then I dove back under the water and started swimming off, looking for that fish.

Bob Sylvester and Mike Cole were laughing so hard they were in tears. But while half of me was fooling around, just being entertaining, the other half of me was dead serious. I wanted to get that damn fish! And I think that's what made it work as a bit for the show. The reality of it.

When we got back to the studio and looked at the tape, we

decided it was pretty funny. So we decided to run the credits over the part where I swam around, looking for the fish.

Later, walking around the NESN offices, I'd hear things like, "Hey, that's the guy who jumped in the lake after the fish. That was a nice four-pounder you *almost* caught." That's when I realized that we had something, and that's what the show started to become known for: unpredictability. It wasn't just about actual fishing. It was more than that. People wanted to watch for the personality. *My* personality. The approach I had to fishing. I made it real. It was as if you were out on the boat with me. The viewers never knew what I was going to do or say next. And most of all, we were having . . . FUN! That was the difference between me and other fishing shows. Fun. And that's exactly what I was looking for.

We got some more mileage out of that little skit, by making it something of a running joke. On the last show of the season, New England Patriots Todd Rucci and Scott Zolack picked me up and threw me in the water so I could catch the fish that got away. And the following season, we had as a guest Heath Irwin, an offensive lineman with the Patriots, and when I missed a fish he taunted me: "Charlie, are you gonna take that? You get in there and you go after him."

"Okay, I'm gonna do it. I'm gonna get in there." I jumped into the lake and a few seconds later I came up, waving the fish in my hand. "I caught it."

Just Give Me the Microphone and Let Me Do It My Way

My favorite singer of all time, hands down, is Frank Sinatra. Frank Sinatra is where it begins and ends for me. I like Tom Jones. I like Elvis Presley. But Frank Sinatra, that's the pinnacle, man. You look at Sinatra and you ask yourself, is he just a singer? No. Does he get up on stage and just belt out a tune? No. Frank

Sinatra *is* Frank Sinatra. People want to *be* Frank Sinatra. They want to walk around with a cigar and a tumbler of Scotch and to own Vegas. That's Frank Sinatra. If you're Sinatra, you don't just go to a nightclub and sing. You *own* Vegas. You walk around with a blond or brunette or redhead, a cigar, a bottle of wine, with Sammy Davis Jr. at your side. You own the town. You're Frank friggin' Sinatra.

It's about being a bigger-than-life personality. People like Sinatra are icons. They're big stars. And that's what I wanted to be. Do not insult me by saying, "It's only a fishing show, Charlie." No. That's like saying, "Frank Sinatra is *just* a singer." Any questions?

3

Will the Real Charlie Moore Please Stand Up?

Okay, now it's time for a little reflection. Don't worry. You won't get too much of that in this book. And speaking of books, who would have thought that the first book I'd ever read from beginning to end would be my own? Anyway, just remember, I am all about having fun. So this won't be long. But I do want to talk a little about my thought process at the time I was trying to get the show going.

First, let's back up a little to when I was at rock bottom, closing Bass Country: I'm a total failure. I want my own TV show. It's an idea that's not even remotely feasible, but I'm entertaining it anyway. Not only am I entertaining the idea, but I'm telling everyone I know about it. Somehow, the more people I told, the more real it was to me, the more it seemed within my grasp.

Then, after a year of hounding people at NESN, I actually got what I wanted. And the first day out there, everything that could go wrong went wrong, but I got through it. And slowly, the show started to improve because I found my voice. Not anyone else's voice.

During the early period, one of the first people I talked to in the industry was a guy named Ted Ancher. Ted had a book out called *Bass Bets,* and he had a regular column in the *Boston Herald,* where he would take some local pro out and he'd write about their favorite spot to fish and their favorite lure. Stuff like that. It was a great concept and his column appeared every Friday.

One day, out of the blue, I called up Ted. All I said was, "My name is Charlie Moore and I've got this five-minute fishing spot on *Front Row* on NESN and I'd like to take you out fishing with me."

Ted was taken aback, I'm sure, but for some reason he agreed to go out fishing with me for the day. It was May 12, 1997, and we went up to Lake Winnipesaukee. We had a great time, and Ted wound up writing a big article on me and the show. Just from spending that one day with me, Ted knew it was going to be something big and, as a result of that article, momentum began to grow.

Now to my point. Eyes up. Pencils down. There are actually fishermen out there who think the success of my show is dependent on me catching a fish. That blows my mind. There's no right-minded person in the world who thinks that anybody can go on stage and be Jay Leno or David Letterman. It wasn't just because Jay has someone writing his jokes for him. It's because he's Jay Leno. Even if you had his writers, do you really think you could get up there and host *The Tonight Show*?

After I got to know Ted, we started fishing tournaments together. It was a lot of fun, but I didn't do too well in the beginning. I'd been more of a saltwater fisherman, so I was just learning how to bass fish. And yet, I'd bump into these guys who'd say, "Sure, you've got your own TV show, but jeez, how many tournaments have you won?" Or, "You've got your own TV show, but do you fish in the Bass Masters Classic?"

Driving home with Ted after a tournament, I'd ask, "Do these people really think that a good bass fisherman can become a good TV host? Is that what these people think?" Sure, it could happen. But it doesn't mean it will. Did they think that because Terry Bradshaw was a great quarterback twenty years ago, that's the reason he's the lead broadcaster for Fox's Sunday football coverage? He's there because he's a good host.

Remember Howard Cosell? Sure you do. He's the guy who had enough balls to tell people like it was. And one of the things he said was that, just because people play a professional sport, it does not automatically qualify them to be a professional broadcaster. A professional broadcaster is a professional broadcaster. A professional football player is a professional football player. Howard Cosell said it himself. He wasn't going to go down on the field and play quarterback for the Washington Redskins because he was a professional broadcaster and not a professional quarterback. So why should someone think that just because they played quarterback they could come in and steal his job?

As we drove home from those tournaments, Ted and I had countless hours of conversation about this mind-set, about where I was going, about what I wanted to do. We even discussed whether I should continue fishing the tournaments or just focus on making a great television show.

I wanted to continue entering fishing tournaments because I loved them, so I decided to do both for a while. Even today, as busy as I am, I still fish tournaments. I've done very well, winning a lot of local tournaments and finishing in the Top 10.

But let's get this straight: Just because people go out fishing, or even win tournaments, doesn't mean they can host their own television fishing show. There's a lot more to it than that—which is what I learned that first year. Before I started, I might have *thought* I could be an instant success, but those first few shows proved that it was going to take a lot of hard work. There was a lot more to it than simply catching fish. I was juggling a whole lot of balls in the air at the same time. I had to teach something about fishing. I had to catch fish. I had to entertain the viewers. And, eventually, I had to sell the show to sponsors, which was, in many ways, the most difficult part of the job. How did I do it? How did I go out and find sponsors? Did someone create that for me, or did I do it myself? Some people think that someone must

Steve Lemoine and me at the first tournament I ever won. Lake
Cochituate, Framingham, Massachusetts. We had 22.5 pounds.

have leaned down from some cloud and cast a spell on me and
that's how I made it. Or they think, "His dad must have owned
NESN. Or ESPN. Yeah, that's it."

I wish my dad had owned the station, but he didn't. People have
this need to justify why they don't have something that someone
else does. It just blows my mind. The truth is, most successful
people, at least the ones with staying power, create their own success. They don't accidentally fall into it. They exploit their strengths
and minimize their weaknesses. And that takes time. And it means
that you sometimes have to be willing to fail. I did. If you'd seen
those first few shows, you'd see exactly what I mean. But I learned
from my mistakes. And what I learned is that I had to be me, not
someone else's version of me.

It's kind of funny how things have now turned full circle from
those days of hanging out with Ted Ancher. Now I'm on NESN,
the largest regional network in the country, and I've got a national

show on ESPN, and I'm really starting to make a name for myself. And still, people come up to me and say, "I caught a bigger fish than you. How come I don't have my own show?" Early in the game, that really bothered me. But now I can live with it, because I've figured it out.

I used to think the same way until I realized that it's not just fishing. It's entertainment. And that's a hard industry to be in.

The lesson I learned from all this is that you can't let other people define you. You can't let them bring you down. If you believe in yourself and what you're doing, just do it. And if you fail, that doesn't mean you should throw in the towel. Tenacity, my friends, that's what it's all about. Tenacity and the belief in yourself and what you're trying to accomplish.

The Three Charlie Moores

Essentially, there are three Charlie Moores. There's Charlie Moore fishing for fun. There's Charlie Moore fishing to win. And there's Charlie Moore fishing for television. In the beginning, I thought I could intermingle all three of these Charlie Moores. But at a certain point, there was a split. Soon, it became time to decide: Did I want to be a professional fisherman or did I want to be the host of a television fishing show?

I made my decision to concentrate on one particular Charlie after a few trips across the country to fish in tournaments. I competed in about six national tournaments in all. I drove to Springfield, Missouri, to Table Rock Lake, and fished in the Bassmaster's tournament on Sam Rayburn Lake in Texas, and one on Lake Martin in Alabama. I didn't do terribly well, but I was getting a feel for it. Remember, up until then, I had never fished outside of New England.

My friend John Naramore financed me, but I still wound up staying at the cheapest motels and eating the crappiest food. But there was one trip in particular that made me seriously reassess what I was doing with my life.

I was making the twenty-six-hour trip out to Lake of the Ozarks, in Missouri. There were lots of family matters still weighing on me. We had no money. I had no direction. I had no college degree. I was putting my family in a corner by trying to fish professionally. How selfish could I be?

I never felt more alone in my life.

There were some guys from New England fishing the tournament out there and one of my friends, Lee Bailey Jr., who ran the Foxwoods Bass Challenge, asked, "What's wrong, Charlie?" Obviously, something was bothering me. For starters, I don't think I'd ever been so quiet in my life. Don't worry, it won't happen again.

"I have a lot on my mind."

"Well, let's go to dinner and we can talk about it."

At dinner, I told Lee all my problems, everything that was bothering me, and he said, "Sometimes, Charlie, it's not all about fishing. Sometimes, you gotta do what's best for you and your family."

"Well, maybe I shouldn't be doing this at this time in my life."

Later, when I got back to my room, I was feeling even more alone. Maybe what made it clear to me that something was wrong with this picture was that, while I was staying in some sleazy, run-down motel, Lee was on the other side of town staying someplace decent.

I called Angela. She and I talked about the kids. We talked about the fact that we couldn't afford food, that I had no direction. Not to mention the fact that I was worried about my brother, David, who had a serious liver problem and needed a dialysis machine. Never, for even a moment, did Angela hint that she didn't want to be with me, and yet I could sense that the gauge on the gas meter was heading toward empty.

That phone call really hurt. Bad. I didn't feel like a man. I felt like I had given up on all my responsibilities. And here I was, checking out rods and reels for the tournament the next day.

The next morning, I woke up and went down to the boat ramp. I sat there a while thinking. About everything.

And then I left. I drove straight through, all the way home.

I remember going through Ohio, smoking cigar after cigar to stay awake. At one point, I put a cigar in my mouth backwards, burning my tongue. Maybe it's time to pull over, I thought, and take a little nap.

When I got home, I hugged my wife. Then I visited Dave and told him I'd always be there for him, along with the entire Moore family, since no matter how much we fight, when it's time to stick together, we do.

My decision was made. I wasn't going to be a professional fisherman. I was going to be a professional TV host. That was the responsibility I took on when I got married and had a family. And by trying to make it as a professional fisherman, I was neglecting that responsibility. It was time to take a stand and turn 100 percent of my attention to television.

And so, my friends, that's exactly what I decided to do. I was going to be the host of a television fishing show. That became my mind-set. And that's how the momentum built. For me, I decided I'd rather win an Emmy Award than a fishing tournament any day of the week.

Don't Worry, School's Just About Out for the Day. So We Can All Go Fishing.

That first season, we didn't have any formula—actually, there never will be a formula for the show, unless you count me as a formula. In the beginning, I guess I was trying to emulate a lot of those traditional fishing shows, but at the same time I knew they were boring and I didn't want to be boring. I wanted to be entertaining. I'm an entertainer. I always have been. But I was also a damn good fisherman. I was fishing tournaments and I was fishing to win. But I was also having fun, and that's what I wanted to translate to the show. I wanted to do a great show that just happened to be about fishing.

When I first started, it was more about teaching people how to fish—and there's still an element of that today—but I also wanted to teach people how to have fun, and because of that the show started to take on a life of its own. People watched because they wanted to see what I'd do next, what I'd say next. And so did I.

That first season taught me a lot. It certainly didn't make me any money. Think about it: Ten episodes. Fifty bucks an episode. That's five hundred dollars a year—I still have a copy of that first check. So, I still had to work, which meant that I had to find a job. And I did. Not only did I keep working for Larry Saggese, but I got a job delivering packages for UPS, as well as a number of other odd jobs.

Year one ran from May to October, and then I was off the air until the following May. That's the way it was for the first three or four years and that really pissed me off, because it meant that I wasn't on TV for something like six months. Yeah, it wasn't about my ego, it was all about the fifty dollars a show. Right.

Let's face it, I liked being on TV. And five minutes, ten times a year, was not going to satisfy that craving.

The Mad Fisherman Is Born

Bob Sylvester remembers how Season Two began:

> That first year, Charlie got one five-minute segment, every two weeks. In the second year, the people at NESN asked, "Do you want to bring him back?"
>
> "Of course," I said. The truth is, nobody really cared—and I don't mean that in a good or bad way. *Front Row* was just a machine. We were churning out four stories a night. They agreed to another season; it was either that or find some other way to fill the gap. But I definitely wanted to do the show with Charlie and he definitely wanted to do them, to the point where he was all over the executive producer and the other people at NESN.

Season Two rolled around and I wrote a nice note to Harry Sinden, the president and general manager of the Boston Bruins and of the station at the time—a nice guy, by the way—pointing out how much we both liked to fish for smallmouth bass. We got a little correspondence going back and forth and eventually I called him and we made a date to go out and fish for the first show of the season. He asked if he could bring Johnny Bucyk with him. Johnny Bucyk? Of the Boston Bruins? Are you kidding?

It was no secret that celebrities were out on outdoor shows. I didn't invent the idea. *The American Sportsman* did it all the time. But this was going to be different, because I was going to be the one interacting with these celebrities. Not some professional TV host who was used to being around famous people. I'm a run-of-the-mill guy. I'm not some phony on CNN or Fox News who'll stick the mike out and ask the stupid questions like, "Are you gonna play tough?" Or, "How do you think the game is gonna go?" Everyone does that. Me? I'm a personality. Combine that with another personality, and suddenly you've got a dynamic situation. Chemistry. At least, that's what I was hoping for.

With guests like Harry and Johnny booked, we decided to make it our first half-hour special. So you were moving into the big time, huh, Charlie? Not so fast. Let's not get ahead of ourselves here, bro. I was still only going to get fifty bucks for it. Just because it's a thirty-minute show didn't mean NESN was going to pay me any more for it. That, my friends, is television.

The show would kick off our second season, so the plan was to take Harry and Johnny up to Lake Winnipesaukee—where else? The special was also auspicious because it was going to be our first two-camera shoot.

The day came, it was late April, and the weather was horrible. Not just bad. Horrible. It was forty-three degrees. It was raining. It was sleeting. The wind was blowing. It was so bad that the precipitation, rain or sleet, was coming down sideways. We had six-foot waves. And remember, this was a lake, not the ocean. I mean, there was no way anyone in their right mind would want to be outside, much less out on a lake, fishing.

And here I am with Harry Sinden and Johnny Bucyk, both of whom are legends up in these parts, and I was *dying*.

But you know what? It didn't bother these guys in the least. We're running around the lake in the boat, going eighty miles an hour, getting pelted in the face with rain and ice pellets, but nothing

seems to faze these guys. What I didn't realize was, this was probably normal weather to these guys. They're Canadians. They're used
to it. This was like summer to these guys. And besides, and I say this
with all the love in the world, they are *nuts.* At one point I said, "I'm
really sorry about the weather," and they replied, "Don't worry
about it, Charlie. We're having a great time."

Yeah, of course they were. They were drinking Molson and
smoking cigars. Oh, yeah, I forgot to mention that Bucyk showed
up that morning with a giant cooler the size of a dining room
table, filled with beverages, smoked salmon, and all kinds of sand-
wiches and brownies. If we were to sink and end up on a deserted
island in the middle of Lake Winnipesaukee, we'd be set for six
months. We wouldn't even want to leave the island. No one
would get voted off. We'd all stay there and have a party.

So, we've got plenty of food and plenty of beverages, but no
damn fish. We were out there for*ev-ah,* and we just couldn't catch
any fish. Allow me to let you in on a little secret my friends: If
you've got your own fishing show and you don't catch any fish,
you won't have a show for much longer.

We were looking for bass, but we would have taken anything.
Anything that hit the line, would have been fine with us. We, or at
least I, was dying to get out of there. But I wasn't leaving without
a fish. So, I started to jump spots. This was a fifty-thousand-acre
lake and we started moving all over it. We were doing eighty miles
an hour and Johnny is in the middle, and Harry is sitting to his
left, and he'd taken his whole rain suit and pulled it over his head
and tied it around his neck.

I'd forgotten anyone else was even in the boat with me, that's
how panicked I was about finding fish.

"You guys okay?" I asked.

Harry said, "We're havin' a great time, man!"

And they were.

We were eating like kings. We were laughing. But still no fish.

Does that mean I sucked? No. It just meant that I didn't know
where the key spots to fish were. Let's be honest, I had no idea

what bass fishing was. Today, I go out there on that lake and I know exactly where the fish are. Back then? No friggin' idea. Now that I've been up there a zillion times, I could have friggin' mono and someone could poke me with a fork in the eye and I could still catch six fish. But back then, God forbid we should get even one bite. I'd figured, hey, we're going to the best lake in New England, it should be easy.

Largemouth bass fishing is the biggest crapshoot of any type of fishing, but guys who are good at it can always catch some fish. It's all about experience. Fishing in different types of weather, different types of lakes, different environments. But I was just not that experienced. Not only wasn't I experienced on TV, but I wasn't even an experienced fisherman.

Don't get me wrong. I could fish. But to pull off the whole "Look at me, I'm a TV pro"—well, that's a different story. If you're having a bad day, you have to adjust. You have to go shallower or deeper. Freshwater fishing is not like saltwater fishing. It's very weather sensitive. There are many variables and it takes a long time to learn all of them. I'm talking weather, water depth, type of lure . . . there are at least eight different factors to take into account. And until you've been in many different types of environments and done some work figuring those things out, you just don't know.

If you're skilled, you can go to the dock and try to wait it out, as opposed to going around the whole lake just hoping to get one fish.

Back to Harry and Johnny. While I was suffering, thinking my career was over, they were having *fun*. Fine. For them. But I cannot possibly explain the pain, the torture of being out there with this guy who's in charge of the entire company, and we weren't catching anything. What made it even worse was that, while I beat my head against the boat, these guys were having the time of their lives.

This was the first show of the season, my first half-hour special, and we weren't catching anything. Eight hours out there and we didn't catch one damn fish. It was unbelievable. I was concerned. Hell, I was more than concerned. I was pissed off. Here NESN had finally invested in two cameras. They were spending more money on the show than they'd ever spent. They were giving me a half-hour instead of five minutes. The big boss is in the boat. A Hall of Fame hockey player is sitting beside him. And what happens? I bomb and leave them at the altar.

I didn't really know these people. I didn't know the ins and outs of NESN and the makings of TV. I was thinking, if I don't come back with a show I'm gonna be screwed. Wait. Forget screwed. My career as a TV star (okay, that's stretching it a little, but you get what I mean) would be over practically before it started. But what could I do? Oh, yeah, that's right, I could go back to my career blowing leaves off lawns.

It got dark, so we turned the boat around to head back to shore. But just as we got to within sight of the boat ramp, Harry, God bless him, hooked a fish. I was freaking out.

"Oh, my God," I cried. "It's unbelievable! We actually caught a fish. I think we're gonna get a show after all."

Harry laughed, turned to me and said, "Charlie, you suck. I'm a better fisherman than you are."

Damn Canadians. But man, they can fish.

When we got back to NESN, that day's experience, especially the end when Harry caught the fish and I went crazy, started to spread through the organization. People began thinking of me as the Mad Scientist type. Listen, I didn't care how they were thinking of me, so long as they weren't thinking of firing me.

The kicker of the story is that we didn't even wind up airing that show at all. How could we? It would have been thirty minutes of me and Harry and Johnny eating in the worst weather imaginable—I don't even know if you could even see anything with water all over the lens—and no minutes of anyone catching any fish.

A couple weeks after the shoot, Tom Caron, who worked for the network, came up with the idea of introducing me as "NESN's Very Own Mad Fisherman." And that's where the name came from, me on the boat with Johnny and Harry, losing my mind, going crazy, mad, nuts. They thought I was having a meltdown, when in reality I was just being me.

That half-hour special with Harry Sinden and Johnny Bucyk was a turning point for me and the show. We really didn't get a great show—hell, we only came back with one fish—but what we got was a direction, a concept, something that was very important for us to have if we were going to succeed.

All You Need Are Friends

During the second season I hooked up with John Naramore, who became an integral part of the entire operation. John owned a restaurant on Lake Winnipesaukee called Wolfetrap, which he was just building at the time. It would open right next to the boat launch we used. He also owned a marina called the Back Bay, where he sold boats. John and I became very close. Financially, he became one of my biggest backers early on. He saw a lot of love in me and he trusted me in terms of being able to accomplish what I said I was going to accomplish, and I wound up spending a lot of time with him. We had a lot of fun and as things moved forward, he actually started to give me a monthly paycheck, which believe me, was something I needed desperately. He also bought me a Ford pickup. John was probably the most significant person in my life at that time. It might have been a different story if I hadn't met John. It's a very emotional topic for me, because he had faith in me.

John was a huge part of my success. He saw the whole picture, he saw the potential. He knew it was going to happen. He could see it coming. So I wanted to return the favor. I started to bring people up to that area and to his restaurant. As a matter of fact, that's where I brought Harry Sinden and Johnny Bucyk when we launched the second season. I even had John do some cameos on the show. I brought people to his restaurant, but I could never pay him back for what he did for me.

Sadly, John passed away a year or so ago. And what I'm going to do here is apologize. It got to the point where I was so busy, flying all over for the ESPN show, that I let some things slide. One day, on my way back from shooting a *Beat Charlie Moore* episode, I thought to myself, "I really have to call John." He'd tried to get hold of me. I remember his message, "Charlie, I want you to come up here so we can have lunch." But I was so busy I just didn't have the time to get back to him. I got home late that night, and the next morning my friend Shawn called and told me that John had just passed away earlier that morning.

Let me tell you, to this day I am so sorry I never got a chance to say good-bye. I know everyone says that, but I just wish I could have had one more lunch with him, just to thank him for all he did for me, for my family, for my kids. Because I was coming from nothing when I first met John. Nothing. And to do what he did for me, to say, "I love this kid. He has so much potential. I'm going to give him a truck." Well, people just don't do that. He helped me get to the point where I could succeed. He opened the cage and said, "Okay, Charlie, now you go out there and do it." He helped me get to the financial level where I could provide for my family. He was always there, as a friend and as a mentor. So, I wish I had one more lunch with him, so I could say, "Remember that time when Johnny Bucyk and Harry Sinden came up . . ." There are so many stories we could tell each other.

And so, let me take this opportunity now, an opportunity I didn't have before, to say, "Bye, John. I love you, bro."

Charlie Moore, You're a Fish

While transitioning from *Front Row* to my new show, *Charlie Moore Outdoors,* I decided that, like Nike and other big companies, I should have a logo. I contacted a close friend of mine, Dave Parzialle, whom I've known since I was eight years old. Dave owned a screen printing company, Skin Tight Graphics, and I told him what I wanted, my vision.

Now, most outdoor shows use a real largemouth bass or something else related to the outdoors for their logo. And hunting shows use guns. But I didn't want that. I wanted the logo to resemble me.

"If I were a fish," I asked Dave, "what would it look like?" Dave sketched a largemouth with a mean face and spiked hair, and put my trademark sunglasses on him. That's how the Mad Fish logo was born. Over the years, it's become the topic of many a conversation between Dave and me—and it's undoubtedly become one of the most notorious works of art he's ever done. It added another element of identity that other shows just didn't have.

I Want My Own Theme Song

One day, I was watching Mike Adams's *Sports World* on TV and, in between commercials, Mike brought a band on the show. I loved the band and the idea, so I contacted Mike and he introduced me to Gary Funchion, whose band was called Dr. Humble. Gary and I became good friends, and I asked him to sit down with me one night and to write a theme song for my show. We played around with some stuff and came up with the lyrics.

Actually, there are several royalty checks going out because people would say stuff like, "Hey, I added the word 'sand.'" Or, "I was the one who said, 'Go to the lake and I'll go fishing with Charlie Moore.'" Welcome to the world of entertainment.

Gary and Dr. Humble recorded the song. Gary came up with the idea of a Jay Leno high-pitched voice, to give it a *Tonight Show* feeling. Actually, we wrote this snappy theme song with that in mind. Over the years, Gary has played a lot of events and, inevitably, people ask him to play the Charlie Moore theme song. So I guess it's worked.

Now I had the logo and the song, and both these elements have been essential to the branding of Mad Fish.

When Larry Met Sally

Early in my NESN career, I caught a largemouth bass.

"Oh, this is a nice . . . ," I began, then paused for a few seconds, looking for some new way to refer to it, just to liven things up a little. "Hmm. Yeah. This is a nice . . . Larry. Yeah. Larry, the Largemouth."

For the next few shows, I periodically referred to any largemouth I caught as Larry the Largemouth, not realizing that the name was starting to catch on with the folks watching at home.

A few weeks later, I was towing my boat to an upcoming shoot, and I pulled into a station to get some gas or, as my friend

John "Topwater" Sloan and me holding some Larrys.

Larry Saggese likes to call it, some "sag," which is "gas" backwards. A man standing there with his family yelled out, "Hey, Charlie, quit playing with your dingy."

No, wait, that's a line from the movie *Tommy Boy*. Man, I miss Chris Farley. I have stolen so many lines from his movies.

In reality, the man said, "Hey, Charlie, you gonna catch any Larrys today?"

I looked at him like he was crazy. Larrys? What the hell was he talking about?

"I watched you catching a few Larrys last week," he said. "Nice fish."

We shook hands, had a few laughs, and then I headed off to the ramp for the upcoming TV shoot. When I arrived, I told Bob what happened.

He looked at me. I looked at him. And I knew we were both thinking exactly the same thing. And why wouldn't we be? We were TV people now. And we knew a good hook when we saw it.

"Okay," Bob said, "let's run with it. From now on, largemouths are Larrys. And you know what? Maybe we should come out with a *Charlie Moore Bass Fishing Dictionary*."

A few weeks later, taping on Lake Arrowhead, in Limerick, Maine, we put together the first installment of my dictionary. This time, I caught a smallmouth bass during the taping.

"This is a nice . . . ," I began, "um . . . Sally. Yeah, that's it. Sally. Sally the Smallmouth."

A few casts later, I caught a pickerel.

"Hey, this is a nice fish, too. Let's call it Pete. Petey the Pickerel."

At the end of the show, I said, "Okay, let's recap. The first fish I caught was Larry the Largemouth. The second was Sally the Smallmouth. And the third was Petey the Pickerel."

Back at the studio, during the editing of the show, Bob put together a graphic explaining the *Charlie Moore Dictionary*. That cheesy thing that took ten minutes!

Years later, during an ESPN taping, I caught a trout. I was just about to put it back in the water when Doug Orr intervened from behind the camera.

"Aren't you going to name the fish?"

"Yeah," I replied. But the only T that popped into my head was "Tommy Vaudo," my pool guy, who also happens to be a male nurse—long story, and we've only got room for one long story here, and that's mine. So, it became Tommy the Trout.

After these shows aired, we received a lot of funny e-mails from people all over the country telling us how they name their fish. I guess it's kind of like naming your car.

Anyway, so long as we were naming things, Bob and I named that day on Lake Arrowhead, "The Day When Larry Met Sally."

With no offense to Billy Crystal and Meg Ryan, of course.

All Good Things Must Come to An End. But That Doesn't Mean Something Better Can't Come from It, Right?

By our second season, the show became more of an entertainment program than a fishing show. The idea was to show fishing as it really was: an opportunity to relax and let your hair down, if you had any.

But by the third year, *Front Row* was beginning to run out of steam. There was less money than before, and some of the staff started to leave. As a result, NESN gave us two five-minute segments per show to fill the time, almost half the episode. That was great for me.

The truth is, no one was paying much attention to us. We were pretty much flying under the radar, which meant that we could experiment more and be a little looser. By the third season, though the show was still evolving, I'd pretty much found my voice.

As Bob points out:

Charlie was great on camera and people finally respected his ability. At least the production staff did. He'd done a good job of cementing a healthy relationship with the people at NESN. He always delivered what he said he was going to deliver. We went out and did our thing, came back, put together the show, and there was no drama, because we didn't complain about anything. And they didn't either. Why should they? We'd get Bruins on the show. We'd get Red Sox on the show. And the show didn't cost NESN anything. All it cost was getting me and the cameras to go out there and boom, a couple of days later, they had a half-hour show. A funny and entertaining half-hour show. A show they were making money on.

By that third year, we were doing a number of *Front Row* specials, which really just meant that they gave me the whole half hour to do my show. There even came a point where I was hosting *Front Row.* I loved it. I'm not sure everyone at NESN understood what was going on, but that didn't matter to me.

For instance, one day Bob and one of the senior NESN producers were standing in the hall talking while one of my episodes was playing on the TV in his office. The volume was turned up and at that point I was on the screen, freaking out. Yeah, I do that sometimes. I don't know why. I just get so excited, I can't help myself.

"Oh, yeah. A smallmouth! Yeah! Woo!" Bob could hear and see me while the producer, with his back to the office, could only hear what was coming from the TV. Finally, he said to Bob, "What the hell is that?"

"Oh, that's Charlie Moore."

"What's going on?"

"Nothing. That's just Charlie," said Bob.

In 1998, NESN finally pulled the plug on *Front Row,* which turned out to be a blessing for me, because it led to me getting my own half-hour show, *Charlie Moore Outdoors.* And that's when things really began to take off. Finally, after three years of being a supporting player, I was going to be a star. Of my own TV show. Life was good.

And it was going to get even better.

The Tournament of Champions

I won my first fishing tournament when I was a kid of about eleven or twelve years old. I was fishing in Winthrop, Massachusetts, my old stomping grounds, at Crystal Cove Marina where my dad kept his boat. I was there with my older brother, Dave. Dave and I are a lot alike: quiet, kind of laid-back. What? We're not?

Anyway, we were down there at the dock and they were having a flounder tournament. It took a while for them to set up the rules and, by the time they did, Mother Nature started to blow, which meant that the waves were growing higher and higher. Yes, the sea was angry that day, my friends. It was really getting ugly. So ugly, in fact, that of the twelve guys entered in the tournament, three of them quit.

Not Dave and me, though. We went to the end of the pier, which by that point was moving back and forth like a roller-coaster ride. Basically, we were just hanging on, trying not to be swept into the ocean. We had a fishing boat rod and a drop line. But almost immediately the fishing rod fell into the ocean. Now all we had was the drop line. As you might imagine, no one was having much luck that day. But, with only a half-hour to go in the tournament, I caught a good-sized flounder. I brought him in and, as it turned out, that was the only fish caught that day. So Dave and I won the tournament, which is something we still talk about today.

So, you can understand why I love fishing tournaments. I came up with the idea for the Tournament of Champions as an attempt to give something back to the local angler, the guys I grew up with, hung out with, and fished with before I got on TV.

The idea was that we were going to fish for large and smallmouth bass, competing for a grand prize of $10,000. The contest would be televised on NESN. Back in the day, there were no real big televised fishing tournaments other than the one on TNN, so this was going to be really a huge thing for our New England fishermen. And I wasn't going to make a dime on it. As a matter of fact, we ended up losing money the first time out. But that's not what it was all about.

I sent out invitations to about eighty guys and the plan was to take sixty of them, one guy to a boat. Despite the $300 entry fee, which would cover our expenses and the prize money, within a matter of days, all the spots were all filled.

We held the tournament at John Naramore's marina, on Lake Winnipesaukee. John "Topwater" Sloan was going to be the emcee.

Let me tell you a little about John Sloan and how he got that nickname, "Topwater."

I met John, who's a few years older than me, one day on the lake when the cocky bastard came up to me and said, "I hear you're gonna have a TV show, huh?"

"Yeah," I replied, not having the foggiest idea who this guy was.

"Well," he said, "we've got a bass tournament here this morning. On this lake."

"Yeah, I know. That's why I'm here."

"And let me tell you something, this is *my* lake."

"Oh, yeah?"

"Yeah. I *own* this lake."

"That's good. I guess I'll see you back at the landing when we're done."

So, I went out there and literally had the day of my life. I could do no wrong. By the end, I had twenty-two pounds. On eight fish! The runner-up had fifteen or sixteen pounds, and guess who that was? That's right, the owner of the damn lake, John Sloan.

But I did the old boy a favor. I let every single boat weigh in before me and because he had the most weight, he thought he'd won. Then the guy doing the weighing said, "Oh no, wait, we've got one more boat to weigh in." That was me. I knew I had him beat, so I wanted to be the last one to weigh in, just so I could ruin his day.

But he took it pretty well. He came over and high-fived me. He laughed and I laughed and instantly, we became best buddies. And we joke about it to this day.

Eventually, I hired John to work with us on the show. He did some of the camera work early on and he drove the boat. He was also in charge of the road crew, making sure that all the boats went where they were supposed to for the show. In the beginning, we didn't actually pay him, unless you count allowing him to use all the boats and lures as payment, which come to think of it was almost more than I got paid for doing the show.

Now about his nickname, Topwater. I like to name everybody around me. It's like I'm in the Mafia or something. There's "Hunter Jim" Kevlik, Larry "Geese" Saggese—you can figure that one out for yourself—Nick "the Slapman" Saggese, because he slaps everyone as he walks by, like, "How's it goin'?" Slap!

John would always fish from the back of the boat. The only thing he ever threw were topwater fishing baits and still he'd catch fish. Now, I'm a fast fisherman. Okay, let's face it. I'm a fast guy. I talk fast. My personality is fast. I throw a skin at ninety miles an hour.

So, I'm in the front of the boat, my throttle is on a hundred. I'm throwing a wake on the back of my boat and he's back there trying to throw a worm out in twenty feet of water. But all John's worm is doing is floating at the top of the water—where else would it be? He couldn't get his bait down there in the water, even if he wanted to. He was in no position to catch a fish, but somehow he'd always manage to catch one and it would piss me off. Hence, the nickname "Topwater."

Back to the Tournament of Champions.

Somehow, we neglected to provide John with a proper stage, where the fishermen would weigh in their catch. When that little omission was pointed out to me, I quickly came up with a solution.

"Okay," I said, "here's what we'll do. We'll put the scale on one of the boats and then we'll put the boat up on the trailer and then we'll have the fishermen come up on the trailer and inside the boat and weigh the fish."

Sounds reasonable, right? But all that stuff about the best-laid plans is true. First of all, John was a big guy and then there was this other big guy in the boat, and then there was me, along with all the equipment. Kind of a tight squeeze. To make matters worse, the wind was blowing so hard, not unlike that day I won the flounder tournament when I was a kid, that it was making the pointer on the scale jump all over the place. So there we are, all this money's on the line, and the scale is bouncing back and forth—ten, nine, ten, seven, ten, five, eight, two, three and a half.

It was nerve-wracking. I was sweating so much I must have lost five pounds that day. Still, it worked out well. The show was a hit, and the tournament brought some much deserved attention to our New England anglers.

Ultimately, the tournament got to be too much work to continue. But it was fun while it lasted. It was exciting to give those guys that kind of NFL stage. NESN aired the show in good faith, and it gave the anglers an opportunity to bask in the limelight—at least for as long as it took for people to change channels or for the tournament to end.

Again, I didn't make any money on it, but what was more important was that I wanted to make a name for myself with these guys, to let them know I was there for them, that I was one of them. The event also brought a lot of fishermen to that end of the lake, which wasn't nearly as popular as the other end of Lake Winnipesaukee. Prior to that, a lot of fishermen never bothered to run the whole lake, so they were unacquainted with that end. Once the tournament introduced that area, a lot of guys started to learn how to fish that end. They found their favorite spots.

I'm Tired of Just Fishing. Let's Do Something Else for a Change.

I am a child of television, from watching Charlie Chan movies on Friday nights with my dad to watching sitcoms because, of course, I love to laugh. Duh! Who doesn't?

Sure, I was the host of a fishing show, but I didn't see any reason why I couldn't combine genres—comedy and the outdoors. So the notion of doing little skits on the show seemed like a natural progression. Bob and I discussed it and he agreed that doing skits every once in a while was not going to ruin the show and that, in fact, it would probably improve it, adding another dimension, giving people another reason to tune in and have some fun with us.

The first skit we did was, I think, in the spring of 1998, and it was for the first episode of the season. The premise was that I would be fishing my usual spot on the lake but, because I was acting a little "mental" and bothering the people around me, someone calls the cops, and I get arrested and thrown into jail.

At the time, we had a friend, a bass fisherman named Dennis Reardon, who happened to be a sergeant on the Framingham, Massachusetts, police force. Dennis put us in touch with the chief of police who said he'd be glad to help us. So, we got the police to pick me up in a cruiser and throw me in the tank. And then we had Tom Caron, who was the host of *Front Row* and is now the studio host for the Red Sox pregame show, come down and bail me out. And then we went out and fished together.

The response we got was terrific. Kids especially loved it, so it opened the door to all kinds of new things we could do with the show.

Life Is But a Dream

I was in a slump. It happens sometimes. Even to someone like me. I'll admit it. Happy? The fish, they just were not biting. And, as a result, I was in a funk. After all, what's the Mad Fisherman without fish? Look, you get a couple of shows where you're kicking the crap out of the fish for two or three hours and then another time you go out there and go a dozen or more hours, until the sun goes down, and you barely have enough fish for the show.

In the midst of this funk, Bob Sylvester came to me with an idea. Usually, when I come up with an idea, we have to do it tomorrow, but when Bob comes up with an idea it usually takes us two years to get around to it. But this idea was too good to pass up. It was yet another way for us to make the show fun, exciting, and to take it another step away from those guys who make fishing look boring, which was something we were always trying to avoid.

"Okay, Charlie, let's make up a little show called *The Dream Show* where you're in a slump and you're visited by three ghosts— Elvis Presley, Austin Powers, and Ted Kennedy"—who, quite frankly, *is* a ghost at this point—"and somehow, together, they get you out of your slump and back to catching fish again."

And why those particular guys? Well, Austin Powers was hot at the time and Elvis Presley is always a crowd favorite and then there was Massachusetts senator Ted Kennedy who is, you know, Ted Kennedy. I would have a dream in which these three showed up and helped me out of my slump. That was the premise, but we didn't write anything out. They gave me the general idea, hired impersonators, and then let my personality take over.

It sounded good to me. We found three look-alikes and we had a little candle-lighting séance session and everyone put their hands together and sang "Kumbaya" and then I went out and caught some fish. It was very funny stuff. And we actually brought the Austin Powers character, who was played by Mike Rydberg—who, in an interesting side note, started his show business career by being a Pee-wee Herman look-alike—back for a couple of other shows.

Is There a Doctor in the House?

After a while, a show, any show, becomes like a family. In our case, it was a traveling family and, like any family, there's bound to be bickering, arguments, fights. You get out there on the water, someone says something, and someone else says, "Shut up!" Of course, it's never me. I'm a sweetheart. Easygoing. Easy to please. It's the other guys, I'm talking about. Yeah. Right.

Anyway, one day we were filming and I said, "Hey, folks, welcome back to the show. Today we're trying to get fish in shallow water. We're going to be looking for lily pads and it'll be tough . . . ," and then, practically before I finish my sentence, Topwater shouts out, "I got one. Over here." And the camera pans over and there's Topwater reeling in a three-pounder. Then, the camera swings back to me and I'm thinking, "You son of a bitch . . ." But instead of that, I said, "You know what, maybe we should have a staff psychologist who tries to help us keep it together."

Later, at a staff meeting—well, a me and Bob meeting—we decided a psychologist might be a good idea, so we created a character called Dr. Howard Fine. We picked the name as an homage to Moe Howard and Larry Fine, two of the Three Stooges. We hired Mike Rydberg, the same guy who played

Austin Powers in the dream sequence skit, to play the part. Of course, out of his Austin Powers costume no one knew it was the same guy.

We ad-libbed the whole sketch, which is what we always do. Nothing on the show is scripted . . . chances are, if it were, I'd just forget the lines and just say whatever came to mind anyway. Instead of a hard-and-fast script we come up with an overview, a theme, and then we say, "Okay, here's what we're going to do." Or, "Here's the feeling behind it. Here's what I want you to say. Okay, go."

And then we go into it.

I tell Dr. Fine that I'm not feeling well, that in the last three or four episodes nothing's coming together. The mechanics are there, I tell him, but I'm still not performing the way I should be.

He tells me I have to get in touch with myself, go back to my roots.

"Go back to when all the fun began, Charlie. You have to get back in touch with your friends. Charlie," he adds, "you have to jump in the lake."

"Are you going to come with me, Dr. Fine?"

"I'm a psychiatrist, not a lifeguard, Charlie."

So, I jumped in and we cut to a scene of me, underwater, with a fish in my hand, and I'm petting it. I let the fish go and, like magic, I'm cured.

But that was the last in-the-water scene I ever did, because it's easy to go to the well too often.

Dr. Howard Fine became a recurring character and, whenever things start to get a little testy, shall we say, we call on the good doctor to help us work things out.

My cameraman, Eric Scharmer, was there, so I thought I'd let him get in a few words here:

> Over the years, Charlie and Bob came up with lots of gags. One of my favorites was during the presidential election of 2000, we did a skit in which Charlie ran for president. We got a

limo and all these people to act like they were Charlie's supporters. It was crazy things like this that made the difference.

At one point, NESN decided to change nights on which the
show was going to air. So Charlie and Bob came up with this
idea of hiring the most well-known moving company in the area,
Gentle Giant. They had Charlie sitting in front of his TV set, with
all his fishing gear, and the movers came blasting in the door,
they shrink-wrapped him and his gear to a dolly, brought him
downstairs, moved him into the truck, closed the truck doors,
and then there was the simple tagline, "Charlie Moore is moving
to Thursday night." As you can imagine, it was very effective.

I never wanted to shoot anything like I was mailing it in. It
didn't have to make sense to me, it just had to be interesting or
eye-catching or outlandish or entertaining, which fit right in with
what Charlie wanted. For instance, one day I went up to Charlie's mansion to get "reads," short clips to take us into and out of
a segment. It was a beautiful spring day and I thought it would
be boring just to shoot the reads around his house. So, I started
them out on the porch and then I actually got Charlie to do the
rest of them as he was climbing up the side of his house, first up
the window, and then ending up on the roof. Frankly, the only
reason I did this was to see if I could screw with Charlie and see
if he'd do it. And he did. But he's great that way. He'll do just
about anything you ask him to do. Of course, when I mentioned
the peak of the roof as the final destination, he said, "Listen,
dude, if I fall off this roof, it's done." And yes, if he had fallen,
there would have been no more Charlie Moore TV shows.

That '70s Show

One of the funniest things we've done recently for the NESN
show was taping an episode with my good friend and New Hampshire guide, Shawn Marzerka, on Lake Winnipesaukee. As part of
the skit, Shawn wanted me to go salmon fishing. I, of course,

wanted to go bass fishing. Knowing that Shawn would be on the lake fishing for salmon, I needed to go bass fishing incognito. Angela and I had picked out some cool outfits at the store. So, I thought to myself, how fun would it be if I dressed up as a '70s hippie rocker with an afro. Actually, I ended up looking more like Sib Hashian from the band Boston by the time I was done with my hairdo.

I began fishing in this funky '70s outfit. I've got to tell ya, it was hilarious not only because of the way I looked, but because the lake was packed that day and every fisherman that drove by looked at me, stared for a minute, and then yelled out, "Hey, Charlie! How are the fish biting?" And here I thought that nobody would recognize me at all, because I looked like Jimi Hendrix.

That day truly taught me just how much people get the show and the zany stuff we do. Although I'm sure being in my orange and green Aubuchon Hardware bass boat didn't help with the incognito part. Oops! Did I just plug Aubuchon Hardware?

Shawn ended up bumping into me and, of course, I felt bad. So we compromised and went fishing for bass, because that's what I wanted to do. Shawn and I were fishing in tight and we were searching for submerged rock boulders and weedy patches of grass. We ended up catching some really nice Larrys and Sallys that day. And to add another level of excitement, there were a couple of guys there from *Boston* magazine and they were doing a huge story about the show in their August issue. Let's just say that the article came out great partly because Shawn and I didn't hold back that day. Or it might have been that '70s costume—I can't say.

Red Sox Win the World Series

For years, we've all heard about the Curse of the Bambino. Now, it was almost to the point where even I started to believe in it. But things were about to change.

And now, I will explain how I, Charlie Moore, lifted my own

curse, the Curse of the Bassbino, and helped the Red Sox win the World Series.

It was an early fall day. Bob Sylvester, John Martin, Chris Martins, Jim Kevlik, and I all headed up to Lake Winnipesaukee, where we were going to do a show. That time of year can be very difficult to catch fish, because the lake was transitioning from summer to autumn.

The day started off funky. First, we stopped at my local general store, Spolletts. They were all out of my favorite beef jerky, which Jim usually picks up for me on the way to my house. At the boat ramp on Lake Winni, I discovered while getting dressed for the taping of the show that my Red Sox baseball cap had mysteriously vanished. I then went to tie on my favorite Lunker City Fleck Spinnerbait and it, too, had disappeared. I turned to John and said, "It's that damned curse—the Curse of the Bassbino."

"I have an idea," John said. "Why don't we do a show where, if we go out today and catch twenty bass, no matter what size, largemouth or smallmouth, just as the Mad Fisherman would call a shoebox full of fish, we will not only lift your curse, Charlie, the Curse of the Bassbino, but we will also lift the Red Sox curse, the Curse of the Bambino."

"Brilliant," I said. "What an awesome idea for a show."

That day was nothing less than magical. We went out there and caught a shoebox full of fish. And at the end of the day we declared it a success. And before the show closed, we told the viewers that we had done it! We'd lifted the Curse of the Bassbino!

That show, my friends, aired in October of 2004. A month later, the Red Sox went on to win their first World Series and lifted their curse—the Curse of the Bambino.

And it's all because of five people: John Martin, Chris Martins, Bob Sylvester, Jim Kevlik, and, yes, me—The Mad Fisherman. To this day, I'm still upset that Tom Werner has not given us our well-deserved World Championship rings. After all, if it wasn't for the show that we did on NESN, the Red Sox might not have won the World Series.

The Codfather and the Creative Process

I think, down deep, it's every man's fantasy to be in the Mafia. At least, it's mine. There are plenty of times when I want to be able to beat people with a baseball bat but not get in trouble for it. Come on. Be honest. You've felt that way, too, haven't you? Like with the guy who cuts you off and beats you out of a parking space. Or the guy who comes back with ten fish to your none. The fantasy of being in the mob is all about doing whatever you want without any consequences, simply because it's your world.

My favorite movies? *Goodfellas, Scarface,* the first and second *Godfathers.* Favorite TV show? *The Sopranos.* Figures, huh? I think you're going to find that most men are right there with me. Remember what the movie was that I was going to rent when I met Angela? You got it. *The Godfather.*

I was up late one night, watching *The Godfather* on HBO, and I started to think about how similar Mafiosos are to fishermen. Fisherman are a secretive bunch—they don't tell anyone what's going on, where they've been, where they're going, what kind of bait they're using. Just like *omerta,* the code of silence in the Mafia. I thought this would be a fun idea, because in all my years of fishing it's still funny to see the reaction you get when you ask someone else what lures they use and what lake or part of the ocean they're on when they're catching all their big fish. They look at you like, "There's no way I'm telling this guy what I'm doing or where."

So, I'm thinking, "How funny is that?" And I start to think about a character whose sole (no pun intended, of course) purpose in life is to rule fishing for the entire country. To go fishing, you'd have to go through him. To get permission to fish a particular lake, you'd have to ask him. And he'd get a percentage of all the lures sold anywhere.

I thought about how cool it would be to try to work in a character like the Godfather into my show. That night, I started to jot down some notes regarding this new underground fishing crime boss.

When I approached Bob with the idea, I didn't see him performing any cartwheels. He thought the idea was way over the top. I didn't. Which meant that we were going to do it.

We had pretty much completed a script, but I still had no name for the character. Before filming the first segment, Bob looked at me and said, "I've got it! You're the Codfather." I was like, "Man, that's money. Absolutely perfect."

That's how the Codfather was born. And you know what? It's been a very positive, popular character for us. People can relate to it. People understand what it's supposed to be.

Codfather Part I featured a great lineup of guys. Geese was played by Larry Saggese and Vito was played by former Boston Bruin Steve Leach. Both these guys did a tremendous job in playing the Codfather's henchmen. Billy the Bass, who was our first victim, was played by Mike Genest.

Larry Saggese, the Codfather, and Nick "The Slapman" Saggese.

Me at two years old in Lynnfield, Massachusetts.

Mom, me, and my sister.

My brother Chris and me as kids in Cape Cod.

My brother Dave and me at my first tournament after we won.

Angela and me at the Mad Fish X-mas bash (2006).

The family: Nikolas, me, Anthony, Kaitlin, and Angela.

Nikolas, me, and Anthony on a family trip to Bear Lake, Maine (1999).

Me in Alabama (credit: Ted Ancher).

My X-mas TV special.

Larry Saggese, me, Keith Kevlik, and Jim Kevlik
during my X-mas TV special.

Bruins legend Ray Bourque and me on a NESN shoot (2007).

DMC, Gary Funchion, and me, shooting an ESPN episode (2007).

Me landing Real Andrew's fish on a NESN
shoot in Alabama (credit: Ted Ancher).

(*Left pag*e): The Mad Fisherman catching a bass.

Gary Rossington, Rickey Medlocke, and me in Florida.

Mitt Romney and me.

Angela in Curaçao on an ESPN shoot.

Angela and me on an ESPN shoot.

Me holding my 14-pound bass in Alabama
on a NESN shoot (credit: Ted Ancher).

Of course, the Codfather was played by me.

Codfather Part I ran about five minutes and was a great success. When trying to write *Codfather Part II,* I found it very difficult because, naturally, I wanted us to outdo ourselves in the sequel. Both Bob and I decided there would be a little bit more of a story line and that we would stretch it a little in length.

Codfather Part II again had many great characters. Larry Saggese (Geese) made a return visit, along with his brother Nick Saggese (Nick the Slapman). Our victim for *Part II* was Johnny Spinner (played by Chris Martins). Johnny Spinner didn't feel like he had to go along with the other heads of the fishing families, played by Bob Sylvester, the Fly Fisherman, and Topwater Sloan. But after a visit from the Codfather, Johnny Spinner saw things differently.

In eight years of doing television, filming the Codfather skits— and now there's a *Codfather Part III*—ranks right at the top. *The Codfather Part I* and *Part II* are both available on VHS and DVD, and soon to be released is *The Making of the Codfather,* which will include all three as well as behind-the-scenes footage.

This, to me, is a perfect example of why I think the show is so successful and why people aren't able to imitate what I do. Because I work on it 24-7. This is who I am. It's like what Mike Myers says about how he created Austin Powers. He was taking a Jacuzzi and he started thinking about this character and it turned out to be Austin Powers. I saw him telling that to Barbara Walters on TV and I could totally relate to it. That's exactly how the creative mind works. I'm always creating a show in my mind. I'm always trying to create something funny. I'm always creating my next idea. You can't have people create that mind for you. You can have them tinker with it, make it better, build on the idea— but they can also make it worse. The real creative talent lies in coming up with the raw elements, like Jim Carrey or Robin Williams do. You give them a direction and they go! And then they or someone else molds something out of that. That's very much the creative process in a nutshell.

Codfather Part III

Unlike *The Godfather III,* we needed to make *Codfather Part III* good. I wasn't going to let Francis Ford Coppola's daughter ruin our sequel. But I did cast my brother, Chris, as Senator Jacques Reelman, a politician totally against fishing. In fact, he held a conference in the town square, telling citizens that we should stop hunting and fishing because people were wasting their time. Instead, they should be out there working, making money. The funny part is that, while we were filming the show—with Angela Angela and my sister-in-law Colleen in the background holding up anti-fishing signs—people were pulling into town square and getting really pissed off because they thought it was an actual rally.

All I'm thinking is, "Are people going to think the Mad Fisherman is attending a pep rally for the anti-fishing people?" But I'll tell you, it was really funny to see people get that upset. I had to tell them, "No, we're just filming a show. We're actually going to whack him later," referring to Chris, playing the senator.

The plot of *Codfather Part III* was that, unbeknownst to the senator, we had secret footage, of him spending a quiet afternoon catching largemouth bass with his friends. The senator is confronted with the footage, revealed to be a fisherman himself, and he changes his stance. Only then is he re-elected.

There was a political message there: What could possibly be bad about taking a kid fishing, or going fishing with your friends? It was a slap at organizations like PETA, who are mainstreaming their message about the abuse of animals.

Now don't get me wrong. I'm totally against the abuse of any animal, or person, for that matter. But come on! You shouldn't go fishing because you're torturing the fish? Give me a break. What people don't realize is that it doesn't end there. They get someone like Pamela Anderson as a spokeswoman. She wears makeup. She wears leather. And that stuff about eating living things. Come on.

Everything you eat is a living organism. You build a house, you "killed" the wood.

It's gotten so bad, PETA tried to stop the Boy Scouts from giving merit badges for fishing, because it was inhumane to the fish.

I was driving in Alabama a while ago and I passed a billboard that showed a dog with a fish hook in its mouth and the line under it read, "Would you do this to your dog?"

The answer is, "No, I would not go fishing for my dog." And neither should you.

Let's Go Fishing!

Now, it's time to go fishing.

I really love to fish. Nothing feels better than when I'm out there on the boat. In the spring, when the birds are chirping, and I uncover that boat, well, if that's all I had, it would be okay. No. Better than okay. Really good.

I can only relate it to the pro athlete who plays football, rolls around the corner, and gets knocked on his rear end. He gets dirt in his face. Grass in his helmet. But he gets up and says, "God, I love this game."

And that's the way it is for me.

It's the whole package. Being on the water for twelve hours, with a thermos of coffee. There' s a chill in the air. There's the smell of wood burning in a stove from a house on the lake.

You get the picture. The love of fishing is at the core of what I do.

There have been times when Bob, Doug, Topwater, and I have spent twelve hours filming a show and then, after returning to the boat ramp to drop off the cameraman, we've turned around and taken that boat right back out there on the water.

Being out there on the lake, or on the ocean, is the best time in the world. No cell phones going off every two minutes, no dealing with executives who think they know how you can make the show better. And no having to look at the numbers on how the show is doing. Can anyone actually figure those things out? If you can, give me a call—but not when I'm out there fishing, please.

Every outdoorsman who reads this book will understand that feeling. It's the little things about the sport that make you feel comfortable: the start of the engine, the sound of the animal life that's out there.

We can talk about one-liners and jokes, the celebrity guests, the wild camera work, the cool music, and the Codfather, but I know that the most important thing is that people see a dude who is extremely excited to be where he is now.

My hobby is my job. And I'm a very lucky man, because not many people can say that.

So, get your rods and reels ready, because now it's time to head out and do some actual fishing.

First of all, I never sleep the night before I go fishing. I love to grab a cigar, go downstairs, and check out all my fishing tackle. "There it is!" As if somehow, mysteriously, it disappeared between now and the last time I went out on the boat. I can't fully explain it, the feeling I have, but I do know I get it every night before I'm going fishing.

The night before heading out onto the water, I spend a lot of time in preparation, checking my rods, switching out bait, putting on new hooks. The anticipation of getting out there on the water is very much like the anticipation on game day, if you're a football player. My brother Chris used to throw up in the locker room before every game. I know. I was there. His little brother, who acted as his trainer. I'd always wonder exactly when it was going to happen. He was so wound up. Because he was thinking about it. I used to have a coach who'd say, "If you don't get nervous before a game, then you're not thinking about it. And if you're not thinking about it, you're not going to win."

Just like Chris, before getting out there on the lake, I start to feel nervous. I feel the butterflies.

But going out there is the reward, the candy, the payoff—going to different lakes, catching Larrys and Sallys, fishing in and out of this country.

Not only do you have to be a good TV host, nailing that punch line every time, you also have to develop a great ability to fish. It's not just twenty-one minutes of jokes and catch one fish. Oh, wait, we've done that. Still, if it doesn't look like I know what I'm doing out there, the show doesn't work. Actually, I've become a better fisherman because of the show, because I've been forced to catch fish.

The one thing that's made me a real good fisherman is narrowing down the wide variety of ways to catch fish. Crank bait, Carolina rig, Texas rig, topwater fishing, power fishing, these are all different styles that many pros are good at.

Adapting Your Style

Let's talk about becoming a better fisherman. The only true way to explain this process would be to take you through the things I've been through. When I first started fishing for bass, there were three people I spent a lot of time in the boat with: Ted Ancher, John Sloan, and Joel St. Germain. These three men have been my fishing partners for the past twelve years. Oh, wait a minute. Let's not use the word "partners." It sounds wrong to me, a bit weird. Let's use the word "buddies." Yeah, fishing buddies. That sounds much better.

Ted, John, Joel, and me. That makes four bass fishermen with four pretty much completely different fishing styles. Having buddies with different fishing styles really can be a huge help toward making you a better fisherman.

Take Ted Ancher, for example. We've both fished Lake Winnipesaukee many times. As I fished with him, he showed me dif-

Joel St. Germain and me in Texas for an ESPN show. I'm holding
a 3.5-pound bass.

ferent techniques that he used with my favorite lure, the fleck
spinnerbait. Up until then, I thought that the spinnerbait was basically a bait that you threw out and reeled back in. Not true. Ted
taught me that different speed retrieves would allow you to catch
more fish. For example, throwing the bait out, reeling it very fast,
and then slowing it down to let the bait flutter, works real well in
deeper water, especially for the smallmouth. You already know
how much I love the Lunker City fleck spinnerbait. But, by fishing with Ted, I learned how to develop many different techniques
to catch more fish with the same lure.

Now let's talk about John Sloan's fishing style. John likes to
fish s-l-o-w. He loves the tube baits and the Fin-S fish, anything
that slows the cast-out and reel-in process down. He did not like
fast-paced fishing.

Now, you know me. I'm the Mad Fisherman, and I can't stand
still for ten seconds. So my style is completely different from John's.

But by combining the two styles of fishing, one being a very slow, methodical way of catching fish and the other being a fast cover-a-lot-of-water technique—what I like to call the seek-and-destroy pattern—you now have the advantage of being versatile.

Now we have Joel, who is one of my closest friends. We've fished many tournaments together throughout the Northeast. Joel's fishing strength is flipping the jig. As we both started to fish together, I taught Joel how to use a rattle trap. Not that he didn't know how to throw the bait. But I taught him how to rely on the bait to catch more fish. In return, he taught me that, when looking for a big fish, you might want to slow things down and be more methodical with the jig.

I'm sure you, too, have a best friend, an uncle, a wife, or a girl-friend who fishes, too. As you fish with these people, watch how they catch their fish. Learn from the people you spend time with on the water. Understand how they catch fish and how they use different lures differently. And if you do, I promise you you'll start to catch more fish.

In short, it's okay to rip off other people's styles of fishing and become successful by pawning them off as your own.

No. I'm just kidding. Sort of. But the bottom line is, work with a professional and you will become more professional yourself.

My Tackle Box

Here are my five favorite baits:

Fleck Spinnerbait This is my all-time favorite. It's very versatile. You can fish it shallow, you can fish it deep. If you're a slow guy, maybe you've eaten a few too many Ho Hos, or you en-joy Dunkin' Donuts a little too much, then you might want to throw out a worm and wait for the fish to come to you. It can work. I've seen it work. But that's not for me. I'm kind of zany. I'm fast. I want to go to the fish, not have them come to me. Am I surprising you here? So, I'm taking the spinnerbait and I'm throwing it in the water, bam, bam, bam! Always looking at my next cast. My bait's constantly in the water. I'm like a quarterback, moving down the field. Moving the chain. Moving the chain. Until he gets to the end zone.

Rattletrap My favorite color of this half-ounce, whipless crank bait is shad. It's very similar to my number one bait, and I especially love using this one in cold water. I can't tell you how many fishermen I've come up to who are throwing rascal worm, slowly waiting for that bite. There's no right or wrong way in fishing, and it does work, but I'd rather go home than fish that way. It takes way too much time and patience. Both of which, big surprise, I just don't have.

Tube This bait can be used for flipping into weed lines and rock piles. It's phenomenal for smallmouth and largemouth bass.

White, Six-Inch Slug-Go, Made by Lunker City This bait was the original soft plastic jerk bait. What I've developed with this bait is a great skipping technique. The weight of the bait allows me to slip it under the dock and then I can retrieve it either by skipping it again or sometimes you can let it sit and flutter down to the bottom, then twitch it, and let it flutter back up.

A Jig and a Piggyback These are great flipping baits for wood and rocks, especially when you've got four or five fish in your boat and you're looking for that big fish. Go to a jig when you have time to dedicate to that big fish, because it's very versatile. You can use it in twenty feet or twenty inches of water.

Bottom line is, you have to develop your own tackle box. There are a lot of lures out there that might work for Jimmy Houston or Kevin Van Damm, but they're not going to necessarily work for you if you don't feel comfortable with that particular lure. For instance, you might prefer a rubber worm over a spinnerbait.

How many of you have that tackle box of lures your grandfather left you? Or the one your mother bought late one night on the Home Shopping Network? If you do, follow these simple instructions:

Step 1. Gather them all up.
Step 2. Head to the nearest trash can.
Step 3. Dump said tackle into said trash can.

What are your favorite lures? When you figure that out, collect them and add them to your tackle box. You don't need to find that secret lure that works, that green, pumpkin thing-a-ma-hoosey sluggo, although you might (and if you do, add that sucker to your box). Go to the store, pick out sizes and colors, and develop that tackle box. Once you do, you'll be surprised how much more confidence you have when you're out there fishing.

My Favorite Places to Fish

Some of the best fishing is in New England and, if you haven't fished there, you're missing one of the finest experiences in life. Of course, Lake Winnipesaukee is my number-one place to fish.

I love Lake Champlain, which is one of the best lakes in the country, when it comes to bass fishing.

New York's Long Island Sound also offers a great variety of fish.

The state of Maine has so much untapped water. There are so many little holes here just filled with Larrys and Sallys. Lake Arrowhead. Big Lake.

Martha's Vineyard is heaven on earth. You can find striper upon striper, as well as plenty of blue shark. Cape Cod is also one of my favorite places for striped bass.

Florida, up and down the east and west coast, offers some of the best saltwater fishing in the country.

Texas has some terrific fishing—and what makes it even better is that it's great to be someplace where everybody loves what you love to do. And that, my friend, is Texas personified.

Lake of the Ozarks, in Missouri, is a fun place. Everybody there has a great boat and even though I've only been there three or four times, I had a great experience every time.

Log on to charliemoore.com or nesportsman.com for other suggestions.

Would You Buy Used Tackle from This Man?

et's talk money. Because, in the end, that's what television is all about.

When my second season began Peter Frechette, who was in charge of *Front Row,* and I sat down to negotiate my salary. Hey, when you get only fifty bucks a show, there's not much to split up, so I couldn't exactly hire any superagents, could I? They'd get something like seven bucks, and I doubt you're going to find many agents who will work for seven bucks.

I went in there with the idea of getting more money, and it didn't take Peter much time to make it clear that I wasn't going to get a cent more than what they were already paying me. I didn't have much to negotiate with—after all, I wasn't exactly bringing in any money, despite the fact that people seemed to like me and the show—but I had a Plan B, and that was some kind of a revenue split.

"How's that going to work?" he asked.

To be honest, I didn't really know because I didn't even know if there was any revenue, much less how we'd split it. But NESN believed in me and I believed in NESN, so I figured that if I could show them I could make money for the show, then I could probably stay on and not worry about being canceled. And maybe I could even take home a little more than fifty bucks an episode because, if you broke it down, what with all the time we had to put in to actually get a five-minute show, not to mention expenses like gas, I was probably making something like ten cents an hour. I couldn't even feed my cat on that, if I'd had one.

Let's set the scene first. At the time, NESN was a "pay to play" network, which meant that you had to pay to get on the network. But this was a transition time when Sean McGrail was about to kick the station into warp speed and I just happened to be on the same train of thought as a lot of the guys at the top. I was looking beyond *Front Row* and I was willing to do all the work as far as sales went, but I needed NESN to provide the gear and the equipment. The people at the top didn't necessarily think I could do anything with it, but Sean knew that I could. He was willing to take the chance on me going out there and making it a success.

Here's the deal I offered them: Whatever commercial time I sold, I'd split with them, after I used it to cover my expenses, whether it was for travel, gas for the boat, or whatever. They agreed, but that's only because they didn't think I'd have a chance in hell of selling any time. I figured, they'd be getting a show they weren't paying for and, although I wasn't going to be getting a salary, I'd have the potential of making a lot more if, and that was a big if, I could actually convince somebody to advertise on the show.

NESN took a chance on a total unknown. The deal would only really work for both of us if I were to hit a grand slam out of Fenway Park.

That's the plan that was presented to Sean McGrail, the new general manager at the time—he's president of NESN now— and, to his credit, he recognized that this thing was going someplace, that it could be a big moneymaker for the station. Basically, the deal was between Sean and me. He was totally on board and believed I could deliver, and that meant a lot to me.

At the time, I was still living in my in-laws' house—I'd been there for ten years, tormenting them with my stuff everywhere, along with all my files. If you ask me now what was in those files, I haven't the foggiest idea. But it sure looked good having them. I had stuff spread out all over my desk, which also had some fishing pictures on it, just so I didn't forget what the hell I was doing for an almost living. And that's where I started my career in television ad sales.

I made so many calls looking for sponsors, I thought my fingers would fall off. The answer was always no. Until one night down in that depressing basement, on what was probably my five zillionth call. I connected with a fishing lure company called Zylas. I gave them my spiel and they actually bought $1,200 worth of time. Okay, they paid in equipment. But it was something. For the first time, I actually had a sponsor. It was enough to keep me dialing.

And it was a good thing that I did because, if I hadn't, I would never have called Lunker City, a Connecticut company that sells fishing equipment and manufactures lures. Somehow, using the Mad Fisherman charm, I convinced the owner, Herb Reed, to sign up for $6,000 worth of ad time. That was a very big commitment for his company, because he was used to just paying in bait. I give Herb a lot of credit because, at the time, this was like a multimillion-dollar sponsorship to me. Herb essentially gave me the opportunity to succeed. It was like hitting the lottery. That one sale, and I'd made more than I made the whole year from NESN.

I'd been working for fifty bucks an episode and now, suddenly, I'd made $6,000! Now, it wasn't as if that six grand was going right into my pocket—remember, I still had a lot of expenses for the show which, in the past, NESN had paid for, but with my new deal, that was all on me. Still, I'd just made a $6,000 sale, and I was freaking out.

It was a real struggle to get that first sale, but what happens is that after you get the first one, the second one comes easier, and then the third is even easier. I even sold time to Marine USA, a boat company, and ended up getting a free boat from them. Well, actually they didn't give it to me, they lent it to me. It was like, "Oh, by the way, I need to borrow a boat for a while. Well, actually, it's like for the whole year."

Meanwhile, I still had the boat I'd bought. I had the boat, but it was the credit card company who actually owned it, since I still owed something like $6,000 on it. But I was able to sell that Nitro-170 and put that cash in my pocket because, believe it or not, I needed to live off that money.

By the end of the year, I had three or four companies signed up for time on my show, so I was doing pretty well. And feeling pretty good about it.

The Sweet Smell of Success—And How to Get It

The key to success is not only tenacity—if you believe in yourself, you can't give up—but also to build on each little victory, each small battle, until eventually you win the war.

That's the way it was with me. And it still is. I sold the show then and I still sell the show today. No one else has ever sold one sponsorship to date, except me. Angela and I do the contracts. And there's a good reason for that: the personal touch.

Basically, in selling time, I was using myself as the product. Sponsors weren't buying time on my little five-minute spot on *Front Row,* they were buying Charlie Moore. From the beginning, I became friends with my sponsors, because it was all so personalized. They weren't being contacted by some anonymous ad agency; they were being contacted by Charlie Moore himself. With me, there was always the personal touch.

People don't usually have that now. Today, there are layers and layers of people to get through before you get to the person you want. You can call a store and you can't even get to a manager, for Christ's sake. So, I think that personal attachment—"Hey, I'm

actually speaking to Charlie Moore, the funny guy on the boat"—
made the difference. It made a big difference. It was, as the old
song goes, "the start of something big."

Something for Nothing? No Way.

In the beginning, I had a misconception of who my primary
sponsors might be. I thought it would be places like lure companies or boat companies. I thought they'd be all over me,
chomping at the bit to advertise on my show. But it didn't take
long for me to realize that they weren't going to be the sponsors who would sustain me. And there was a good reason for
that.

These big-time lure and boat companies weren't ponying up
the cash. Instead, they were letting the fisherman use their products for nothing. Basically, it was like building a house for no
money.

It didn't take me long to realize that these companies were
making out big time with these TV anglers. They would be giving these professional fisherman a memo boat, which was basically like giving them a presold boat. It was like telling them,
"Use my boat for six months, and then I want you to sell it for
this amount. And by the way, if you can't sell it for that amount,
you owe me this much money."

Are you kidding me? It was the biggest joke in the world. I felt
bad that people were doing these deals and losing money. I know a
professional fisherman, and I won't mention any names, but he's one
of the biggest names in the industry, who was losing $1,500 every
time he got a boat and then sold it six months later. Because you
could never sell a used boat for the amount of money they were
asking for. They were taking a $30,000 boat, lending it out, and then
saying, "Once you sell it you owe me $26,000." Ridiculous! You
drive the boat off the lot, you lose four grand. So these guys were
actually losing money just to be in a boat. And yet, for some reason,

they were proud to run around with this big neon logo on it thinking they were big, bad fishermen.

Meanwhile, I was trying to make a living, trying to pay a mortgage off, trying to make this a profitable venture for me. While everybody else was trying to call themselves a professional fisherman, I just wanted to call myself a successful businessman.

A lot of these anglers think they're going to become a professional fisherman by calling the boat company, calling the lure company, and getting them to sponsor them. Well, that's not going to happen. That's why I eventually turned my attention to companies like Eastern Propane and Oil and Aubuchon Hardware. I still had a great connection with NASCAR and fishing fans, the outdoor fan base, so to speak, so even though they didn't sell fishing products, I knew they would do well advertising with me. Guys like Herb Reed, although still a fishing lure company and in the industry, still really believed in me and knew I was different. And you know, Herb doesn't pay me much more than he paid me in the beginning, but I'm still loyal to him and people like him. I'll never forget that he took a chance on me. And believe me, there's no loyalty in this sport. Hell, there's no loyalty in any sport. It's all business. It's all about making money. These sponsors have been whoring around with professional anglers, using them for virtually nothing. And when they don't need you anymore, they throw you away. I wasn't going to fall into that little scheme that they were running. Yeah, I picked up on that one real quick.

So, I started to shift gears. I looked at the Fortune 500 companies—people who had money, people who weren't related to the sport of fishing. I was the first one to start going after those companies.

Sometimes, the Postman Rings More Than Twice

It was October 2000. I was down to my last few bucks. My family and I were living in Wolfeboro, New Hampshire, down the street from Lake Winnipesaukee. I went down into my little office and got really down on myself. You know, the usual: What am I going to do? How am I going to get this to work? At the time, the show was doing well, but to pay all of my bills, professional and personal, it was still very tight. I had just built this new house and we were all happy. But after all the plumbers, carpenters, and painters had left, the dust settled. A few months had gone by and I realized that I might be over my head a little bit here.

My son Anthony came down and asked me if I wanted to throw the football with him and my other son Nikolas.

"Sure," I said. "But first, could you please go get me the mail?" Anthony came back with the mail and handed it to me. As I looked through it, I saw a flyer for a company named Aubuchon Hardware. Up until that point, I had never heard of them. I flipped over to the back and, to my surprise, they had something like 146 stores. I called one that was near me, asked the gentleman where their headquarters

Anthony Moore #18, Nik Moore #24, and me, the head coach.

was, got that number, then called and asked for the person in charge of television and marketing. That's when Mike Mattson stepped in.

"Hello, Mike," I began. "My name is Charlie Moore." And the rest, as they say, is history. It turned out they saw a market for their hammers and nails in all the carpenters who fished. Smart. Very smart.

I signed a deal with Aubuchon Hardware two weeks later, and we have never looked back. It truly has been a great marriage between the two companies and I can't thank Mike Mattson and the Aubuchon company enough. But the funny part of the story is that there was no super-agent or great marketing plan on my part. It was just my son Anthony going to get the mail and bringing back a flyer of a company that would become one of his father's biggest sponsors.

And then there was Eastern Propane and Oil. And Ernie Boch Jr., who represents Subaru. Ernie and I taped a couple of custom commercials that dealt with the outdoors but were really selling Subarus. That's the future, as far as I'm concerned. That's where I'm going to continue making my money. Not from Stratos boats. Not from some lure company, other than Herb Reed. Listen, if I had a lure company calling me right now offering me hundreds of thousands of dollars, I'd tell them to shove it. I would.

Wait! Hold on! Someone's calling me right now. Okay, I take that back.

Bottom line, I sold myself to the sponsors. I convinced them to buy a piece of me. And when you buy time on one of my shows, you're not just buying ads. You're buying the whole real estate. You're landing on Boardwalk *and* Park Place, when you invest in me. That's the difference between me and other shows.

The whole pro fishing world is a farce. These large companies treat it as a hobby, and yet they want to make it into a true sport. But you're never going to get that until you pay people, until you take care of the people who are in the sport. Recently, I signed a six-year deal with Aubuchon, which is a phenomenal commitment for them. But they're going to get their money's worth, I can promise you that.

Show Me the Money

If you want me to do a commercial for you and use your bait or lures, then pay me. Pay me! The biggest part of my success was creating a television show that showcased my talent. But once the show was over, I'd switch gears. I'd go into Jerry Maguire mode. I am not Charlie Moore. I am Jerry Maguire and I'm selling myself on the phone. I can do that better than anybody. Not only can I fish. Not only can I host a show. But I can run a business and kick some ass.

I always oversell. Myself. The show. The product. It doesn't matter. And when you oversell then there's no problem getting re-signed. When you undersell and get overpaid, then you're going to have a problem.

Honesty is important, too. I've never told anyone any lies. I've never promised anything I didn't deliver. When I tell you I'm going to do something, then I do it. And I'll do it ten times more than anyone else. And I'll do it ten times harder than anybody else. I work 24-7, 365 days a year. I eat, sleep, and drink my success. So don't tell me there's no pride in what I'm doing.

And if you want to cry because you're just sitting there watching the game and not being in it, then you might as well pack it in. You're the one who needs to push yourself. It ain't my problem. My problem is to make sure I'm working as hard as I can. So, if you're asking, "How did he get that show?" Or, "How did he find that sponsor?" All I can say is, are you kidding me? Do you really think anyone's going to give you something for nothing?

Football players work. They work out in a gym. They work out in the field. Baseball players are professional athletes. They work at what they do. They have to deal with pressure all the time. People think it's easy. It's not. Success breeds success. Some doors open because you just open them. But the next couple of doors open because you keep on pushing. You don't stop in one room. You move on to the next room.

I'm happy to be where I am. But you can't stop working, just because you've arrived. You keep on working, so that people keep tuning in, keep having a good time, keep laughing. People love the show. They embrace the show. But when the show's over, it's all about business.

I'm calling my sponsors all the time, asking, "What can I do for you?"—to the point where I'm good friends with these guys now. And that's what I want. Because I want them to know who they're spending their money on. You have a problem with me? Don't call my agent. You call my cell phone. I don't care if it's eleven o'clock at night, I'll answer the phone, and I'll get right to the problem, and then we'll move on. And to me, that's the key to success in this day and age. Everyone's hiding behind a lawyer. Or their business manager. Or their agent. Are you kidding me? You've got something to say to me, you call me on the phone. I'll be the first one to tell you what time it is.

Now It's Time for a Commercial Break

Now you gotta remember, in the late '90s commercials about fishing products were just that—about as straightforward as you can get. "Here is my fishing lure. It catches big fish. Buy my lure." That kind of commercial.

After the show on NESN started to get some staying power and I signed a new deal with Aubuchon Hardware, Mike Mattson and I decided to start creating customized commercials geared around my personality. So, I created an ad campaign for Aubuchon Hardware announcing that they were the official sponsor of outdoor games. See, Southwest was the official sponsor of the NHL, Bud Light was the official sponsor of the NFL, and Nike was the official sponsor of MLB. Well, heck, Mike and I said, let's make Aubuchon Hardware the official sponsor of outdoor games everywhere.

Up until this point, I was just running a sponsor's standard commercial that they supplied to me. In my head, I was thinking, what a great way to brand myself with a company like Aubuchon Hardware. So we created a series of commercials that were extremely funny and had nothing to do with fishing or selling hardware. But, like the Super Bowl ads, the funniest and most entertaining were the ones people talked about after the game. Aubuchon and Mike, as well as Bob and I, knew right away that these commercials were really working. So, we didn't end it with the Aubuchon Hardware sponsorship. I wrote a commercial for Teva footwear that was extremely funny. It started off with me as a caveman walking barefoot along the shoreline, trying to spear a fish. I stubbed my toe, then the commercial cut to me in a canoe (shot in black and white, like it was in the '50s) stepping into the water with some old dress shoes. Then we cut to the present with my bass boat coming up to the shoreline and me jumping out of the boat landing in the water with my Tevas, lifting my foot up, and saying "Ahhh, Teva!"

Throughout the years, these kinds of commercials have become just as much a part of the show as the actual show itself. People tune in to see the new commercials. Recently, I've shot some really funny ones with Ernie Boch Jr. for his car dealerships, as well as for Chuck Clement of Eastern Propane and Oil. I feel like this has made the show more successful—having creative commercials. People who are watching a TV show sometimes run out of the room during commercial breaks. The hope here is that when they're watching my show they won't be running out, because the commercials are just as entertaining as the shows themselves.

So if you're a fisherman reading this book and asking yourself how to get sponsored, the answer is that it's not just about catching a fish. It's about wearing many hats. Being a good fisherman is important, but being a good creator, being a good TV host, and being able to create catchy concepts, are all part of the key. To my success, anyway.

This Is What Makes It All Worthwhile

Let me tell you a story to illustrate why this is all worthwhile to me.

In twelve years of TV, I've never missed one show. That's through laryngitis. That's through fevers. I shot one show, with Drew Bledsoe, with a 103-degree fever. It was brutal, but no one ever knew.

Anyway, I woke up one morning a few weeks ago completely congested in my chest. It felt like I was at death's door. Angela had let me sleep because there was an ice storm the night before. I finally woke up at 10:30 AM and I pretty much felt like somebody had kicked me in the chest. But I had to be in Boston by noon for a big meeting with some sponsors.

So I made it to Boston to meet with the executives in charge of sales for Goodyear in Dallas and a New York advertising sales company. We were there to talk about selling my ESPN show, *Beat Charlie Moore*. We met at a really nice steak house in Boston. As a matter of fact, it brought back memories because it was a couple doors down the street from where I used to take Angela out to eat.

The waiter came over to take our drink orders and one guy said, "I'll have a Coke." The other guy said, "I'll have a Coke." But when it came to me, I said, "I'll have a bottle of wine." What the hell? I wasn't paying for it. Besides, I could have a Coke anytime.

So, I was having a little glass of red wine and the headwaiter, his name was Joe, came over and said, "I don't mean to interrupt you, but I have to tell you that I don't fish, but I love your show."

"Well, thank you very much, Joe," I said.

"And I want to tell you, my mom had cancer. She was in a lot of pain for the last several months. And the only time she ever smiled was when she watched your show." And then he went through a list of individual shows that she loved. It was un-friggin'-believable.

That just about knocked me out. Here I was, sitting there, looking at this guy who'd just told me this about his mother, and all I could say was, "You'd better bring me another bottle of this, Joe, because it's gonna be a long day, bro."

Meanwhile, these guys from sales had no concept of how emotional that was for me. I took a sip of my wine, put it down, and said to these guys, "Okay, do you have a stat for that? Do you have a survey for that? Do you have any graphs or charts for that? Can you measure that?"

The answer is, you can't. You can't measure emotion. You can't understand what effect certain things have on people. I feel a sense of responsibility to people. That's more important to me—what that man said to me—than anything you can imagine. His mother, who has now passed away, spent the last years of her life watching my TV show.

These people continued to look at me, and then they went about their business. But I was a vegetable for the next hour. As I continued to drink my bottle of Beringer, trying to get over the congestion in my chest, I kept envisioning this woman watching my show and laughing. Being in a comfort zone. And that, my friends, is really what the show is about. People watch it and feel good. It's fun. It's entertainment. It makes you feel *good*. That's what it's all about.

This kind of thing, though certainly not as emotional, happens to me every day. It might be in the form of an e-mail (I get five to ten e-mails a day of people telling me a story—sad, happy, glad, bad, mean) about how they would like me to take somebody in their family fishing. Whether it's for their fiftieth birthday, or it's for a police officer who was hurt in the line of duty. And the one thing that person wants to do is to have me take him fishing.

The really bad part of it is, I walk away feeling like, "Wow, am I one of those people who just don't respond to their fans? Am I one of those celebrities who's become so big they can't even do that anymore?"

The reality is, I can't do it. I can't take ten people a day fishing. But I'm just trying to give you the big picture. I'm not just Charlie Moore the fisherman. I'm also Charlie Moore the entertainer. Does a guy like Joe care about the eight-pounder I caught? No! He cares about how the show affected his mother who didn't crack a smile until the show came on. He told me he bought all my tapes and he TiVo'd the show, and she'd watch it for like three hours and then go to bed. That's the impact I have on people.

Hey, just today my e-mail guy called me—yes, I get so many e-mails I now have an e-mail guy. Are you kidding me? What's the world coming to when someone like me has to have an e-mail guy? But I get so many a week that I can't possibly read them all myself. So, I've got a guy who answers it for me. And he gets eight, ten people a day who want to go fishing with me. He doesn't know how to respond. And the truth is, neither do I. What do I do? What do I say to them? Do I say, no? The only thing I can do is say, "Hey, I understand, I really wish your father well. I'm sure he was a good police officer. I'll send you a T-shirt and a sweatshirt—something." I'm one of those guys who has to do something.

But I want to tell you, that story from Joe really impacted me. I won't think about that for a while, and then every now and then it'll pop back into my head. To me it's all about attitude. People don't know it, but there is a deep side of me. A passionate side. That's why I get pissed off so easily. People who get pissed off are passionate. People who walk around letting everything roll off their back, they just don't have that passion.

And how does this relate to this story? Well, personality is what people enjoy. It's what they like to watch. It shapes how they feel about you. It makes them want to get to know you.

That's why this is not just a fishing show. It goes a lot deeper than that.

Angela, Kaitlin, Nikolas, Anthony, and me in Maine (1997).

The Real Charlie Moore

I am not just the guy you see on TV. Yeah, that's a good part of me, but it's not all of me. There are some things you don't know about me, things you couldn't possibly get from watching my show.

For instance, I love being around my family.

Nothing means more to me than my family. A lot of people I meet need a Ferrari to make themselves feel good. They need a $40,000 watch to make themselves get through the day because that means they're important. They need a million-dollar home to live in 'cause they're the man and they're better than anyone on the street. They want to keep up with the Joneses. You can take away my Corvette, my watches, my house, you can take away all that, I'm still the Mad Fisherman. I'm still who I am. That stuff doesn't make me. I like that stuff and, sure, I need some of that stuff just to have some fun. But it doesn't complete my day. Angela and my kids complete my day, as well as all the things I've done in my life. One thing that I'm most proud of at this point is the fact that I'm still able to coach football to my kids. I get more enjoyment out of coaching football to my kids and their teammates than anything I do. And I take these kids—all walks of life—and I'm able to mold these kids into fine young men, and I really have taken pride in that. I've impacted these kids personally.

Here I am with two television shows, and I've got no time to say anything to anybody other than agents and lawyers and the media. Yeah, I'm all over the place and yet I find time to make sure that I'm flying in and out of practice, going to the kids' games. I'm buying equipment and I'm writing play books out. And you know, I really get into that.

But I tell my kids one thing—and I want this to be perfectly clear: "We're down here for one reason. We're down here to win football games. We're not down here just to have fun." Because when you get into the real world it's not about just having fun.

Anthony, Kaitlin, Nikolas, and me with a 3-pound smallmouth bass.

And if you believe that crap, then you're going to be about as blind as a fish out of water. Believe me. They wouldn't have win-and-loss columns in the newspaper every Monday if it's all about having fun. Nobody does a press interview after the Super Bowl and says, "We lost, but dammit, I did have lot of fun." No one ever does that. It's all about winning. And when you win, you have fun. And when you win you feel a sense of accomplishment. I tell this to my own kids and I tell it to my football teams and I also preach it to myself.

There are two kinds of people in this world—there are the people who play the game and there are the people who watch the game. I always say to the kids, "Which one are you going to be? Are you going to sit on the sideline and bitch about what the guy should have done? Or are you going to get in the game, keep your mouth shut, and kick some ass?"

I'm in the entertainment industry, the most cutthroat industry in the world, and here I am busting my ass. I walk into the super-market and people come up to me and say things like, "Hey, how come you went out with Ted Nugent?" Or, "Hey, do you really like Lynyrd Skynyrd?" It seems like everybody's got something to say. But guess what, I'm playing the game and they're watching the game. Now you tell me, who's having more fun?

Here's a word from Angela:

> Charlie has a bigger-than-life personality, both on and off the show. What you see is what you get. He's crazy and extremely emotional. He's like that no matter what. He's also a very passionate person, no matter what he's talking about or what he's doing, whether it's fishing or coming home talking to the kids about their education or their sports. He's such a passionate person that he tells the kids that that's how they have to be, passionate. Like education. He's always telling the kids that they have to be passionate about education because what you do now affects what you can do later on. Our older son, Anthony, is a freshman in high school right now, and I have to remind him

that his grades are going to affect his choice of colleges. "If you want to go to BC, then you can't get C's. You really have to think of your grades now." So Anthony has to have some passion in his schoolwork or he can forget about his first choice of a college. That's how Charlie is, passionate in his business but also very passionate about the kids and what they're doing every day.

He also helps around the house. When it's time to cook, we've had people tell us we flow nicely together in the kitchen. He knows how to get a roast ready while I'm doing the salads and sides. And he never says, "Oh, God, I'm so tired of cooking, why aren't you cooking for me?" He cooks every single night that he's here and he even vacuums once in a while.

One thing that most people don't know about Charlie is that he really has a soft side to him. He is a very sincere gentleman. On the show he's so crazy and funny, but he really is very sincere. You know that he loves you—I know that he loves me and the kids to death because he's always talking about us. And he really shows his emotions. He doesn't hide anything. And I don't know if that comes off on TV because he's so zany. But he really does care about people.

ESPN's Beat Charlie Moore

I had a real good following in New England thanks to NESN, but I was looking to expand my horizons. The only way to do that, to go national, was to hook up with ESPN.

I started leaving messages for Dan Bowen of ESPN, telling him that if he really wanted to have a different show on ESPN, he should give me a call. I left like a hundred messages for him and he never called me back. I don't know why. And how come he never picked up when I called? Oh, yeah, they have this little thing called Caller ID. I guess that might explain why my phone wasn't ringing off the hook.

But he couldn't ignore me for long. The way I heard the story is that, one day, he went into a cafeteria and saw people laughing. He asked them what they were laughing at. They pointed to the television and, lo and behold, what's playing but one of my shows. So, I guess he dug through those messages and called me in for a meeting. I was on my way back from Alabama on a shoot when I got the call.

"Hey, what took you so long?" I asked.

We both decided that we didn't want a carbon copy of *Charlie*

Moore Outdoors. Of course, he didn't. He spent the first hour telling me how bad the production was on my current NESN show. So, at that point I was pretty clear he wanted something different.

Dan and I finally reached a contract agreement for an ESPN show. Winnercom, which was based out of Tulsa, Oklahoma, was going to be the production company for the show. I negotiated a base contract for a one-year, twelve-episode deal, something that ESPN doesn't really do. But to tell you the truth, having my name in the title on national TV was worth almost as much as whatever I was going to be paid.

The first person I had contact with at Winnercom was Tom Dooley and, after talking with him several times, he got a good idea

Doug Orr and me during the first ESPN
episode, taped in Cape May, New Jersey.

of what my personality was like. The concept for the show we worked out was for me to fish against professional anglers, entertainers, and regular Joes from all walks of life. The challenge would be something on the water and something off the water. I liked it. In effect, it was combining a lot of the things we already did on *Charlie Moore Outdoors,* while adding a little something extra to it.

He assigned a producer named Doug Orr to produce the show, to be called *Beat Charlie Moore.* Once I hooked up with Doug and we'd discussed what we were going to do, we both agreed that we were really tired of watching shows that just consisted of twenty-two minutes of fish being caught. And believe me, I love to fish. But my professional career is not my hobby. My professional career is what I do for a living, which is to entertain people, to make them laugh. This is what I'm interested in doing, not just catching fish.

This was my opportunity to push the envelope, to use techniques I couldn't use on the NESN show. To be honest, although

From left to right: Ryan Moore, Doug Orr, me, and Bob Sylvester. During a Texas shoot for ESPN.

I love Bob Sylvester, we often clashed about the direction of *Charlie Moore Outdoors*. Bob's theory is always, "If it ain't broke, don't fix it." My theory was, "You can always make it better." Look, you make great chili, but who's to say that if you added a little more cayenne pepper, it wouldn't make the chili even better? That was my argument with Bob. But with Doug, it was a whole other ball game. He was excited by the prospect of experimenting a little. He liked the idea of doing MTV-like camera work and editing. He liked the idea of using music more creatively. He wanted to shoot the show so that it looked as good as a feature movie. In short, he was willing to take chances. And I liked that.

The first episode was shot during the last week in August 2003, and was scheduled to air Saturday, January 2, 2004. We were going down to Cape May, New Jersey, and Doug figured he'd try to pull one over on me. It almost worked. Nice try, Doug:

> When we first decided to do the show, I ordered some Charlie Moore DVDs off his Web site because I didn't really know anything about him. Before I met Charlie, we'd had about ten conversations, so all I knew of him was as a result of watching the DVDs and talking to him on the phone.
>
> The day we flew up to meet him we pulled up into his driveway and I thought he'd be all excited, like, here's ESPN coming to do our first show. My cameraman, Ryan Moore, and I get out of the car and there's Charlie, going nonstop, and it wasn't even about us, it was about his son's football game that he'd just coached. I'd never heard anyone talk that fast or that loud in my entire life. I'm originally from California, but I grew up in Oklahoma, so I'm a little more laid-back and not use to the fast, loud-talking bit. At that moment I realized that, whether the camera is on or the camera is off, that's Charlie. What you see is what you get.
>
> And that was the beginning of a long friendship.
>
> The first show we scheduled was with his sister, over in New Jersey. He didn't know what we were going to do—we kind of

sprung it on him the last second, and he was a little shocked. She actually challenged him through the Web site and he didn't know anything about it, so I thought that a great way to kick off the deal would be to have him fish with a member of his own family.

On that first shoot, anything that could have gone wrong went wrong. The trip to Cape May, New Jersey, was a real ordeal. We had to pick up a cameraman in Atlantic City, and we were four hours late. Once we got to Cape May, our credit cards weren't working, the camera equipment wasn't working, and the microphones weren't working. So, I'm sure in Charlie's head it was like, "Okay, here's the big-budget ESPN crew and nothing's going right."

But on the outside, he was taking it pretty well. You know, it was like a first date. We were both kind of getting to know each other, feeling each other out. Now, of course, I hear about anything that goes wrong. But back then, I didn't hear about it. Charlie was used to doing a show on a shoestring budget when we first started.

Once we got on the water things started to improve. The great thing about Charlie is he's just a walking sound bite. What I discovered was, you tape everything because you never know what's going to happen. A lot of those beautiful, funny, really compelling moments happen when they're not planned. We don't stage much of anything with Charlie. We just turn the cameras on and go. I'll feed him a thought every now and then, but other than that it's just on autopilot.

And his sister really whupped him that first show. She whupped him good.

Welcome to the Juliana Moore Show

Yeah, the surprise was that I was going to fish against my sister Juliana. They set the whole thing up without telling me. A lot of people think we set up all the shows, and sometimes we do, but mostly, because of time constraints, everything is pretty much un-scripted. This one was *definitely* unscripted. Of course, when we rolled into her town, I'm not an idiot, I kind of figured out what was going on.

Doug omitted one other "little thing" that went wrong. I al-most got killed.

We checked into the hotel and Doug and Ryan were upstairs on the fourth floor of the outdoor balcony pushing the equipment down. Meanwhile, I was downstairs with Bob Sylvester, talking on the phone. All of a sudden, I heard Doug yell, "Look out."

Instinctively, I stepped back a little and this huge camera comes tumbling down and lands within a couple of inches of me. Evi-dently, while they were pushing it, the camera hit a bump and fell off the top floor, nearly hitting me on the head. Probably would have killed me, which would have made that our first and last show for ESPN. No wonder Doug wants to forget about it.

My sister and me during the first ESPN episode,
taped in Cape May, New Jersey.

Let me tell you, I was really excited about this episode. Not just because it was my first one with ESPN, but also because I was meeting this milestone in my life with my family present, including my mom, who has always been one of my biggest supporters throughout my life. She has been there for me through good times and bad, so to have her there, along with Angela and my kids, really meant a lot to me.

Oh, by the way, did I mention that I'm my mom's favorite?

As far as the actual contest with my sister, well, let's just say I *let* her win.

Okay, okay, my little sister beat me. Is that what you want to hear? And Doug and the rest of the crew loved it. In fact, they loved that she whipped my butt so much that on the little promo they used for the show, there she is screaming into the camera about how she beat me. It's like her big claim to fame, and believe me, she's still on it. You know, like the true Moore that she is, your fifteen minutes of fame stretches out into your forty-five minutes of fame, if you know what I'm saying.

But listen, I had other things to do that day. It was our first episode, so I was worried about the cameras and the crew, not about beating my little sister. The next thing I knew, Doug was saying, "Hey, Charlie, you might want to be worried about the competition, because you're down something like eight to one."

I was like, "Oh, my God, I'm losing eight to one to my sister!" At that point I leaned into the camera and I said, "I love my sister. But like, I'm down eight to one to her. No way."

I came all the way back to tie her and then she caught the last fish to beat me. So yes, my little sister beat me. Happy? And let me tell you, to this day, deep down in her heart, my sister actually believes the name of the show should be *Beat Juliana Moore*.

But hey, nobody takes Charlie Moore down without consequences. Yes, I got her back in the end. Doug and Bob Sylvester were at my sister's restaurant, Bayside Pizza, and they knew I was a little sour about her beating me on the water. That's when Bob came up with an idea for something called *revenge*.

Let me back up a little. The challenge was that if, on the un-likely, very unlikely, chance that I lost, I would have to cook pizza for my sister and Angela at my sister's restaurant. So, when Bob said, "I have one of the big flounders we caught during the show in a cooler outside," I knew just where he was going with this, and suddenly my frown turned upside down.

"Yeah, Bob, that's a great idea. Go get me the flounder."

So, yeah, I cooked them their pizza, and then I came out with my apron on and said, "Here you go. One large cheese pizza—Mad Fisherman–style." Plop. I slapped down that pizza with a big ol' flounder on it.

The Mad Fisherman's Flounder Pizza.

Reaching Critical Bass

That first show aired on a Saturday in January at 9:30 in the morning. As soon as the show ended, at ten o'clock, my friend Steve called. I looked at the clock: 10:02. Man, that was quick.

"Charlie. Just watched the show. Great show. Loved it. Loved it."

"That's great, Steve. Thanks."

"Yeah, the verdict's in."

"And . . . ?"

I couldn't quite make out what he was saying.

"Speak up, Steve."

He stumbled a little more.

"So, what's the feedback."

"Well, you ought to go to this Web site, bassfishing.com. Check the home page."

So, I hung up the phone and went to the Web site, a site, by the way, that I didn't even know existed. It's now 10:07. My mouth dropped open. There were something like nine hundred to one thousand postings! I'm not kidding: nine hundred to one thousand! The show'd been over seven minutes, bro, and already I had a thousand postings.

Now, I decided to read some of those things right then and there. As if my head isn't swelled enough. But some of the postings aren't exactly what I was expecting. I expected something like, "That Charlie Moore, what a fisherman!" Or, more likely, "That Charlie Moore is the best entertainer since Frank Sinatra, and we don't mean Junior."

But they were actually a little bit different. More like:

"Charlie Moore sucks!"

Or:

"This show stinks!"

Or:

"Who the hell is this guy and what does he think he's doing?"

I couldn't read anymore. I was getting sick to my stomach. I went from feeling like Marlon Brando, stepping out of the air-port, wearing a Tommy Bahama shirt, chomping on a cigar, feel-ing great, "Top of the world, Ma!" to that little guy on *Fantasy Island* going, "Da plane! Da plane!"

That's okay. I just had to adjust my outlook a little. Gotta catch my breath. I couldn't possibly suck as bad as all that. Man, I was a big hit on NESN. I'd conquered New England. How could this be happening?

But it didn't end there. The phone calls and e-mails started to come. I remember getting phone calls from a few diehard fisher-men, telling me, "Charlie, the show really stinks." A friend of mine, who was on the NESN show, called me the day the show aired and told me, "The reaction is in. America doesn't like the Mad Fisherman."

You'd think I'd be totally depressed about what was going on, but I wasn't. In fact, after a day or two I actually started feeling pretty good because I realized this was what success was all about. Success breeds naysayers. People were talking about me, good, bad, or indifferent. This, I realized, was just part of the game. This wasn't the time to get upset. This wasn't the time to cry. There's no cry-ing in football. Get your ass up off the ground, let's go, let's go.

The other thing is, in truth, it wasn't that many people had a problem with me. It's just that I'm the kind of person where if there's one or two people who don't like what I'm doing, I over-react. Let's face it, I want everyone to love me. And, on my NESN show, they did. This was new to me. And it took me a little time to adjust.

But I'm not going to lie to you. It was a very difficult time for me. There were three thousand posts on the Web. My friends were calling my cell phone. It was like a tidal wave. But the news wasn't all bad. And a lot of my close friends and fans loved the new show.

A month later, in February, I still hadn't fully come to grips with the way the show had been received, but I was asked to headline the Worcester Sportsman Show, which is the biggest sportsman show in the Northeast. It's run by Paul Fuller, who's become a great friend. He was the first one to ever to let me come in and promote my show, back in 1996, when my boat actually got stuck in the door. Anyway, it was my first public appearance after the airing of that first *Beat Charlie Moore,* and I thought I was going to get lambasted. I thought people were going to come up to me and say, "Why are you doing this? Why are you changing the show?" I was very nervous, because I'm all about respect and reputation. We don't make TV shows to make people uncomfortable. I want to entertain people and to put a smile on their faces.

I remember pulling up in a limousine and seeing this huge line out the door and I said to Chris Martins, my friend and personal assistant, "Oh, God, look at this line for the sportsman show."

"No, Charlie," he said. "That line's for you."

I got inside and it was mobbed. I was supposed to do a three-hour appearance and a seminar, from 10 AM to 1 PM, but I was there till 6 PM. I signed autographs for six, seven hours straight. I got very few bad comments and that's because the majority of my fans, the people who love TV, understood what I was trying to do.

What we were trying to do was to change things, and some people have a real problem with change. We did it with the NESN show and we were out to push the envelope even further on ESPN. Up until I came along, outdoor shows were instructional, not personality driven. What I wanted to be was more along the lines of a Tim Allen driving the show. I wanted it to kick you in the jaw. I wanted it to look like it came off HBO, not PBS. I wanted it to be an MTV show airing on ESPN's Saturday morning block.

I understood that the traditionalists would look at me like I had seven heads. That was fine. I didn't care. I just wanted to help create a new generation of outdoor shows. A Jay Leno–style show dealing with the outdoors. A hybrid. Something that was not only instructional, but also entertaining. Here that? En-ter-tain-ing!

I'm not taking away from any of those other shows, but you watch them and they're not funny. They teach you how to fish. They do a good job of that. I wanted to make my show truly unique. And that's what these "critics" didn't understand.

Despite the fact that I knew I was on the right track, after the storm of criticism sunk in, I started to experience doubts—which, as you know from reading this book, was a fairly new experience for me. I started second-guessing myself. Maybe the show's not right. Maybe it's too much of an entertainment show and not enough of a fishing show. Maybe I should make it more like the other shows.

I started wavering, doubting myself. Dan Bowen and Doug Orr tried to reassure me.

"It is a great show, Charlie. "

"The majority of people watching want a little variety."

"This is who you are, bro. This is the real Charlie Moore."

"Stay with it, bro. We love you."

But still, I started to lean on Doug.

"Maybe we should do more fishing. Or maybe it should be more of a mix."

"Dude," he said, "you're a TV guy. You're so talented. You've got to run with it. We knew what we were trying to do. We were on the same page. We were trying to capture the real experience of going fishing. That's what we were trying to do."

I'm not proud of this, but my initial reaction was to turn my anger and frustration on Doug. And then on Dan. I was constantly calling Doug and Dan four times a day, just so they could tell me how great I was.

Doug didn't want us to change because he wanted to highlight the whole experience, the Charlie Moore lifestyle, combined with the fishing, because he thought it was more entertaining that way.

Meanwhile, it was very stressful on me, my family, Angela, my kids. I started to have the feeling that I'd been at the pinnacle of my career and then, wait a minute! I'd have to start all over again. I went into a little bit of a funk.

The truth is, the show had so much exposure on worldwide TV—ESPN is the largest sports network in the world—I just wasn't ready for it. It's like after you get married. Everyone's asking, "When are you going to have kids?" And you answer, "When we're ready." But when are you ever totally ready for an experience that you can't possibly understand before you get into it? After nine years of success on NESN, I thought I was ready. But obviously, in January 2004, I was totally unprepared for the amount of attention that I got.

And yet, the show was, by all accounts, a rousing success. ESPN was looking for some great watercooler talk, and they got it. The show also got great ratings. We even had great e-mail response in terms of numbers. "Hate him." "Love him." "The show stinks." "The show's awesome." That meant people were watching. But I was in my own little bubble.

So, I stayed with it—of course, there was never any real doubt that I wouldn't. And by the halfway point of that first year, the pendulum started to swing. People started to get what it was: a show for kids, fathers, and grandfathers. A show that was really about how to have fun while you fished.

Beat Charlie Moore was to me what fishing is all about. The success of the show had a great impact on ESPN. Suddenly, they started to see the style of the show and they said to themselves, "This is the future of ESPN outdoors."

We included bloopers in the show. We were the first to use split screens on a regular basis. Never done before on outdoor shows. We used characters like the Blue Dolphin, who gives me orders as to where I go to fish. By the way, he is real. And to this day, I don't know who the voice is on the other end of the phone.

And you can gauge the enormous success of the show by how many techniques and gimmicks we use that are now starting to be copied nationally and locally. For instance, the other day I got a call from Doug who told me to watch *The Scott Martin Challenge,* where the host challenges another pro at fishing, mano a mano. Great concept. Sounds kind of familiar, though, doesn't it?

Boys' Night Out

When we started the ESPN show, it was a blast for me, like a guy's weekend away. I would show up at the airport and everybody knew me. I'd be carrying my tackle bag and I'd get to the airport screener and he'd say, "Charlie, do you mind if I go through this?" And I'd say, "Sure." He'd open it up and he'd find four issues of *Playboy,* four decks of cards, poker chips, and, oh yeah, there'd also be a fleck spinnerbait.

We were ready for a party, but we weren't doing drugs—it wasn't like a rock and roll party. We'd get this beautiful suite and we were calling up for room service and being treated like the movie stars we wanted to be. I was just sitting around with the boys: Doug Orr, Ryan Moore, John Lee, Jim Kevlik, Bob Sylvester, the whole crew, and we're playing poker till three, four in the morning. And then it was like, "Oh, yeah, we've got to get up at five to do a show. I forgot about that. You in or out?"

I'll let you in on a little secret. I enjoy my time on the road. I enjoy my friends, who happen to be the guys I work with. I enjoy having a nice $100 bottle of wine sitting around, and I enjoy smoking a $15 cigar. It's so much fun. Could life get any better?

Doug has something to add:

> The first season was great. It was a real breath of fresh air for me because I finally had somebody with an attitude and a personality that I could edit and mold my style around. I like to edit more MTV-style, as opposed to having two brothers sitting in a boat going, "Oh, that's a nice one." I want my longest shot to be no more that ten seconds, which is unheard of for outdoor programming. That fit in exactly with what Charlie wanted to do. So, I think it was a nice match. And I don't think that was a coincidence. I think someone saw Charlie's work and knew me and said, "Putting these two together could work." And I think that's what Charlie was looking for, too. Someone who understood him

and his style. For me, it was like having a clean canvas for the first time in a long time.

Charlie gave me plenty to work with and the first season was great. It was probably my favorite season just because we were feeling it out and we didn't know where our ship was going. We were just out there having fun doing what we wanted to do. Take the Todd Rucci show, where we fished from a pond. Charlie gets down there and refuses to go to the lake where Todd's used to fishing. Instead, he says, "Let's just stop at the first water we see. I don't care if it's a lake, a pond, or a friggin' puddle." So, they find this little pond and start fishing it. It's one of my favorite shows. It was really well shot, it was funny, and we caught a lot of fish. But the show sticks out because that's not something you see on TV in your usual outdoors show. Nobody has a personality like Charlie's, and that shows in just his walking around a pond fishing. And it was a real competitive show, too. People

Bob Sylvester, Todd Rucci, me, and Sal Malguarnera
on a NESN shoot (1998).

like to see competition. In life everything's a competition, whether you're racing home from a restaurant to see who can get home first—my kids and I do that. With Charlie, it's all about having fun. It's like little kids making up games. Like using different lures to catch a fish. That's all it is. Fun.

If It Ain't Broke, Don't Fix It:
Beat Charlie Moore, *Season Two*

Having to deal with national exposure was a milestone for me. I'm not going to candy-coat it—as I said, the reaction was mixed, as opposed to my NESN show, where over 99 percent of the reaction was positive. But the ratings were very good, and the watercooler reaction was great. To me, that meant the show was a success.

The real disappointment didn't come until six or seven months later, when ESPN tried to make some changes to make the show "better." I thought they were making a mistake by listening to some purists, some people who knew nothing about television, nothing about entertainment. Why change things when you're receiving as many if not more e-mails than any other outdoors show? To me, we had this proven commodity and until that point no one had screwed around with Doug, Ryan, and me. We did everything. No one else got their hands in the cookie dough.

So, here's what it felt like to me: "Hey, Charlie, you kinda suck, but by the way, here's a two-year deal."

I was confused. You're great. You suck. Charlie, you stink!

Charlie, your show's no good. Charlie, we love you. Up and down. Up and down. I knew it was all part of the negotiation process, but it was still very difficult, because I never let anyone tell me I'm no good. Let me reiterate: *People think that because they can catch a fish they can have a show on the largest sports network in the world!*

I don't listen to negativity. Everybody's a Monday quarterback. Shut up! How many downs did *you* play in high school?

Am I frightening you? I apologize. Don't worry, I'm sedated now.

I told them, "This is my price. You want to do the show, fine. You don't want to do it, fine." They knew I had the talent. Our first season of *Beat Charlie Moore* was great. A big success. They knew the show on NESN kicked butt. And don't think that NESN's constant airing of my show didn't go unnoticed by ESPN. They knew everybody was making money. And I knew I was in the right game. I was on the greatest sports network in the country. I was also on the greatest regional sports network in the country—owned by the Boston Red Sox! I knew I was good. What was the worst-case scenario? I wouldn't make my base contract and I'd go back to doing what I was doing on NESN. Hey, that wasn't a bad scenario at all. I could live with that, bro.

If there's one thing I learned as a kid it was, once you've made your bed, you've got to lie in it. So I wouldn't obligate myself to do a show when I wasn't happy with the terms.

So, we made the deal, but Year Two almost turned out to be a catastrophe. Not that the viewers ever knew that. It wasn't my fault. It wasn't Doug Orr's fault. It wasn't Dan Bowen's fault. The truth is, we can all share the responsibility for what happened. We met at the Mohegan Sun—we wanted to have some drinks and some food and do a little gambling and talk about Season Two. I think it was Dan who said, "What do you think about throwing five thousand dollars up for grabs?"

It was during the time of all the reality shows, like *Survivor*, with people winning fistfuls of cash, and I was thinking, "Maybe this'll take the show to a new level. Bump the ratings up a half or even a full point."

But what happened was that we took something that was natural, wanting to beat up on someone and have fun while you do it, and added money to the mix. In the past, it was all about bragging rights. "I caught the biggest fish." "I'm the best fisherman because . . ." Now, it was all about the money. Or at least it seemed that way.

What we didn't realize is that, when we added the prize money, the show got too cutthroat. People were chewing my head off, because too many of those $5,000 prizes was a lot of money. Suddenly, all the fun was sucked out of the show.

The truth is, we got blindsided. And it was a case of miscommunication. Dan simply wanted to add $5,000 prize money to spice things up a little and we thought he wanted to make it this competitive game show kind of thing. In other words, we got the impression from Dan that he wanted it to be this cutthroat game and frankly, I was totally uncomfortable with that. I really don't like making fun of people on national TV. I make fun of people, sure, but I also laugh at myself. And I always let people know I'm just kidding, that it's just a joke. But with this new show, how do you do that with $5,000 on the line? If you have the answer, let me know.

Season One was so much fun, playing poker, eating some good food, touring the country, meeting some great people, fishing, catching big fish, catching small fish, and having a great time. But Season Two turned out to be very different. Here's an example of what I mean.

Rob, a military guy from Virginia, e-mailed us and we chose him to be our first guest fisherman. Turned out, he was a good guy, but he wanted my head on a platter. He wanted to win. He wanted the money. And I don't blame him.

So, I went down there and I brought $5,000 of my own money. That's something most people don't understand. That was *my* money. If I lost that five grand, I was losing *my* five grand. People think ESPN was giving me the money. Wrong-o! That was my money. It was part of my deal that I'd be putting up the cash prize.

Now remember, we were under the impression that we were going to have fun—even with the prize money—because Season One was such a hoot and a holler, which showed on TV.

So, I went down there without ever seeing the lake first. Rob came over the next morning and he was ready for blood. He was so ready, he could hardly give me a handshake. And why? Because the show now had this tournament feel to it.

We went out on the lake and Rob was just handing me my ass. All morning, I didn't catch a damn thing. Lunchtime comes and I'm sick. I can't eat anything. Rob's already caught five fish and he's sitting there and saying, "I think I'm going to become a touring pro."

Yeah, and I think I'm going to go postal.

Doug came over, took one look at me, and said, "What's wrong, Charlie?"

"I think I'm gonna freak out. This dude really wants to win. Game on. This is a much different show now. We're not in Mayberry anymore. This is the Bass National Classic. This is the Super Bowl. I'm down five fish to none. I've got three and a half hours to go and I haven't got one fish. Not one. I haven't had a bite all day."

I go out there and I throw the fleck spinnerbait, my go-to spinnerbait, the whole country knows it, and I get a nice-sized fish. Then, I get another one. Now I've got two. Now, there's about an hour and a half left. I'm at the north end of the lake. Rob's calling from the other end of the lake. I don't know what I'm going to do. I've got two fish, he's got five. I looked over and there was a bunch of trees and a long channel. They were cypress trees and they were sticking up in the channel. I said, "It's getting late in the day, and I see this big, protruding cypress tree. God, please let there be a fish there."

I trolled over there, skipped a spanky, a plastic lure bait made by Lunker City. I got one! I've got three fish now, with about half an hour left. Then number four. Oh, my God, this is coming to-gether! It's like driving down the field for the game-winning field goal! It was hopping. "This guy ain't gonna win. This is my day. No, he ain't gonna win! Four fish and a half hour to go. And I'm gonna get myself another fish."

The next tree, nothing. There's one more tree. "Give me a nice two-pounder, please." The cameraman, John, is sweating. He had his rally cap on. He's yelling, "We're gonna do this. We're gonna do this!"

Now, I'm coming back! I'm coming back and I'm gonna beat this guy's ass. Bam! A two-pounder. I run to the camera. "Yeah!" I throw all my rods down. I tie them to the boat. I look behind me, "John, I got good news and I got bad news. The good news is we got our five fish. The bad news is, I'm gonna put this boat in high gear and we're gonna go about eighty miles an hour, so you'd better tie yourself down, because if we hit something, you're gonna go for a ride. We'll make it buddy, we'll make it."

I turn the engine on, I turn the boat around, and I hit it. Eighty miles an hour. I was just hanging on that steering wheel, white knuckles and all. And I hit the open water, I was gunning that boat. It's 2:59. The weigh-in was at three. Rob was sitting on the dock—he was in five minutes early. He turned to Doug Orr and said, "All I can say is he'd better not be late, or he'll be disqualified."

And just as the guy said that, Doug looks up and around the corner—"Waaaaaaaaaaaaaaaaaaaaaaaa." Here I come. I got there at exactly 3 PM. Rob weighs in his fish and I weigh in mine.

I beat him by five ounces!

Rob just left. He was pissed. And why shouldn't he have been? He'd just had five thousand bucks snatched out of his hand.

We thought that was the show, that tournament emotion, that Dan Bowen and ESPN wanted. So that's the way Doug cut the episode and the others we shot right after that. They were all coming out like this bad-assed tournament show. Oh, Charlie's gonna lose, but he wins at the last-minute kind of show.

Right before the air date, Dan called up and asked to see a rough copy of the show, but we already had the final copy, so we sent that to him. He watched it and called Doug and said, "Doug, what the hell is this? Where's the charm? Where's Charlie being funny? Where's the laughter?"

Doug and I went into freak-out mode. We didn't know what we were gonna do. We'd shot six shows and they were all cut like this one. Because we thought that's what they wanted.

Can you spell c-a-n-c-e-l-l-a-t-i-o-n?

In the end, we kept that show pretty much the same. And then, in order to "fix" the other shows we'd shot, we added a few jokes, and cut the episodes a bit differently, so they were a little more fun and a little less cutthroat. Then we intermingled the shows so that we wouldn't have two intense ones running consecutively. It kind of worked. But the five grand never made it fun for anyone—the guys who lost were really pissed.

And the irony was, the TV audience never knew anything about all this. Since we were able to put a lot of the fun back in, along with that tournament feel, they loved it.

So, we made it through, but it was a good lesson for us. For Season Three, we put the fun back in and it was another successful year. The next season, we learned our lesson and it was like anywhere from a dollar to five hundred bucks, anything we felt like and bragging rights. Biggest fish, a hundred bucks.

We certainly dodged that bullet.

Everything Is Bigger in Texas, Even the Fish

I went down to Texas with Joel St. Germain, one of my fishing partners, to have some fun, which explains the poker chips we brought with us. We went down to meet a guy named Wayne Pruitt. Wayne was a good guy but he came into the cabin where we were staying and started talking some serious smack. "We're going to kill you guys. We're really going to put a whupping on you."

Meanwhile, I'm looking at him like he's crazy. I'm just down there to take in some sun and relax. But hey, fishing is fishing and a challenge is a challenge, so Joel and I decide to rise to the occasion and, besides, I figured it would make for a great show.

Wayne and his friend picked the lake, someplace they'd fished many, many times, so I'm sure they thought they really were going to "put a whupping" on us. But it got real cold, down into the forties, which is very cold for Texans, and as it turned out, that's the best thing that could have happened for us. Because these guys just did not know how to fish in the cold.

We came up with a really cool concept. There were two small, separate lakes right near each other. We decided that we'd each fish one lake one day and then we'd swap and fish the other lake the next day. That's one of the cool things about the show: you can make up these little challenges and have fun.

These guys, who were great guys, by the way, really thought they were going to win. Meanwhile, Joel and I were rubbing our hands together and saying, "Okay, bro, we're going to smoke these guys into oblivion, okay? We're going to run away with this one. But let's not make it too bad. After all, we're guests down here . . . and they've probably got shotguns in their trucks."

We went out day one and I caught, among other things, a five-pounder, and Joel caught a bunch of fish. It was incredible. The thing is, Wayne and his pal just couldn't relate to the cold weather. They were using different techniques from us and couldn't adjust them. We came in that day and they had maybe six pounds worth of fish and we had eighteen. The next day we just totally ran away with it.

When these guys watched the show, they obviously thought, "Hey, I can beat him on my home lake. I've fished it four hundred times in the last two years and he's never even been here." But what they don't understand is that they only fish one lake, where I fish the entire country. What they don't realize is that the thing about *Beat Charlie Moore* and *Charlie Moore Outdoors* is that it's made me one hell of a fisherman, because I've fished in adverse weather conditions at all times of the year. Hey, bro, I'm on the water while you're at work!

The A-Team

It was Season Two of *Beat Charlie Moore,* and keep in mind that there was $5,000 in cash on the line. Again, this isn't ESPN's cash we're talking about, it's *mine.*

Doug had come up from Oklahoma and we were at my house reviewing several of the tapes that had come in from the challengers. One tape that stood out was from a couple of guys from Alabama. They called themselves The A-Team, a.k.a. Mark Wolfe and Derek Thomason. While Doug and I were watching the tape, we were laughing our butts off. The A-Team was cracking us up.

Doug said, "These guys would make for a great challenge."

The concept was, the A-Team versus me and my fishing partner of choice. Doug asked if I was in.

"Absolutely," I said.

Doug asked who I was bringing in to help kick some bass, and I told him that I was bringing Angela. We both looked at each other and started to laugh.

Now, don't misunderstand me. Angela is a good woman and a great mom who takes care of everything and everyone in the house, and, yeah, she likes to fish. But to bring her down to Alabama with $5,000 cash in my pocket up for grabs—well let's just say that it was a big gamble.

I knew right away I was in trouble when Angela and I started to pack. She asked me if she should bring some books to read on the boat, what should she wear, what the weather was going to be like, things like that. Meanwhile, I'm worried about other things, important things, things that might keep that five grand in my pocket. Any fisherman reading this book will realize that the toughest thing about fishing far away from home is bringing the right number and the right selection of rods, reels, and lures. It's a real pain in the neck to figure out what you should or shouldn't bring. You're always afraid of leaving that one secret lure behind on the kitchen table.

We were going to fish Lake Jordan in Alabama, and I got down there a day before anyone else. I got a map, but I was only able to spend three hours on the lake, and I was not allowed to talk with anybody at all regarding how to catch fish there. Much to my surprise, Lake Jordan wasn't much of a lake. In fact, it probably should have been called the Jordan River. But by studying my map properly the night before, I figured I wanted to travel about forty-five minutes south and make my way into the back of the coves to look for largemouth. Meanwhile, I knew the A-Team would be looking for big spotted bass.

Guess what? I didn't catch anything during my three hours of pre-fishing.

Angela flew in late that night and we all got a good night's sleep after eight hours of poker. We met the A-Team at the lake for an 8:00 AM blastoff. I told Angela to get ready for her ride from hell, that is, the forty-five-minute trek to the cove where I thought there would be plenty of largemouth bass. Much to my surprise, when I got to the back of the cove, the water had dropped about two feet. A lot of the wood that was submerged in water the day before, wasn't submerged now.

I knew I was gonna be sticking with two lures: my favorite lure, the Lunker City fleck spinnerbait, and a three-eighth-ounce Ya-baby jig trailed with a Lunker City Ozomo bait. Angela and I both fished hard for several hours, but we didn't catch anything. After all, the playing field had changed overnight.

At the halfway point of the day, we met up with the A-Team. Mark and Derek said that the fishing was awful and that they didn't catch anything. In truth, I thought they were sandbagging Angela and me. I decided to go back to where I felt I could get at least a few bites. I never once, in the six hours, stopped fishing.

Not for a drink of water. Not for a piece of beef jerky. Not even for a cigar break. I kept pitching and flipping that Lunker City fleck spinnerbait until I was either going to catch a fish or my arm was going to fall off. I came into one little corner of a cove where there was a stump about two feet from the shore. I turned to my cameraman Ryan Moore and said, "Get ready. Here comes fish number one."

I pitched that bait just a little bit beyond the stump and rolled it right over the top of it, and just as it passed by the stump—wham! I nailed a nice largemouth bass. It was definitely over two pounds and it definitely jumped and then it spit out my spinnerbait. Angela, doing the whole nice wife thing, kept on saying, "It's okay baby, it's okay."

I let it go for a few minutes and then I completely came unglued and started yelling and screaming. After all, this was about four hours into the tournament and I had just lost a two-pounder at the boat. After a few minutes, I apologized to Angela for yelling at her, so she did what every other wife in America would do. She put her rod down and lay down across the seats and started to read a book. Man, did that piss me off.

About thirty minutes later, I saw a similar stump. Would you believe that pretty much the same exact thing happened? They always say that bad things come in threes. So rather than tell you the whole long drawn-out version, I'll just let you know that I lost a third fish about ten minutes later.

So, with about two hours to go, I had lost three keeper fish that would've given me about six pounds. Let me stop right here and remind you that I am actually filming a TV show for ESPN with Angela, and we aren't getting any fish in the boat. Now I want to make the show fun and entertaining, but I also want to catch fish and to win. Obviously, you can't win without any fish, so it looked like I had to pick up the pace. With about one hour left in the tournament, I pitched the fleck spinnerbait about four feet from the boat to a log that was in the water. And guess what? I finally landed my first fish—a two-pound Larry. With about forty-five minutes to go on one of my last casts, I caught another two-pound fish.

Angela and I threw the fish into the live well, locked down the rods, and got ready to scream back to the weigh-in. Mark and Derek had an extremely tough day as well, weighing in only one fish. Angela and I ended up winning with about four pounds.

Not only was this show great fun, but it also made me feel a huge sense of accomplishment in that I went down to Alabama with Angela and $5,000 and, against all odds, came back to Boston with a "W."

As a footnote, Mark and Derek, who are really great guys, actually fished Lake Jordan two weeks later and won a big tournament. My guess is that they were throwing a Lunker City fleck spinnerbait.

Lamar's Tours

I first met Lamar Cox when I was filming an episode for Season Two of *Beat Charlie Moore* against Scott Sweinhart of Melbourne, Florida. Sweinhart hosts a show called *Hot Spots* and it was my job to go to the stickmarsh and beat him. Although I ended up winning, I really kind of didn't, because the fishing was really, really tough. Boy, how many times have you heard that line? "Should've been here last week. The fishing was great."

Sweinhart was a great guest and the show was a lot of fun. But before the crew left to head back home, Lamar issued a challenge to Doug Orr and Doug agreed on my behalf. See, Doug loves to take me out of my element. I guess that's pretty funny. At least to him, it is. So, about seven months later, we headed back down to Melbourne and did a Season Three show with Lamar Cox. This was not going to be your average show, my friends. The thing that was so unique about the show was that I was going to be catching bass from an airboat.

Now, I had never been on an airboat before, so I truly was excited about going seventy miles an hour across the water in one of these bad boys.

We were gonna go on a gator hunt. Yup. That's right. You heard me: a gator hunt. And I hope you're sitting down reading this—and why wouldn't you be, come to think of it—because to top things off, we were gonna go frog gigging.

All right, let's start off with the fishing. Lamar took me way, way into the backwaters. I had no idea where we were. And I can honestly tell you that I have never seen so many gators that big in one area in my life. When we started fishing for bass, every time a tree would move or a bird would fly away, I would jump about a mile. Being from Boston and all, we don't fish around too many gators. I mean sure, you gotta worry about being whacked while you're fishing the Charles River, but you don't have to worry about gators.

I'm a pretty good fisherman. I pride myself on being able to fish hard and always come up with something, but I truly didn't think that we were going to catch anything. There were too many gators. I remember hooking on a white six-inch Lunker City Slug-Go, another favorite lure of mine. I twitched the bait on top in the back of a cove, and then there was this huge swirl and the bait was gone. Let's just say that it wasn't a bass or pickerel. So, yes, I was freaked out and Lamar was loving it, as well as Doug. Oh wait a minute. Let's talk about Doug. What's he doing in all of this. He's sitting up on the top where the driver sits on the airboat smoking a Marlboro Red, basically out of harm's way. I don't think I was the only one out of my element.

As the day progressed, we caught bass off the secondary point, using small spinners. The ones that Lamar sold me for $50 a lure. You know, the same ones that you can get at Wal-Mart for $2.99. I ended up catching six or seven bass. Lamar caught a couple of bass and a couple of brim.

Well, I won the bass fishing and now it was time to relax and wait for the frogs to come out. So Lamar suggested we go to his cabin and eat the brim and wait for darkness. Did I say cabin? I meant more of a shack.

Lamar drove even farther into the swamp. And in the middle of all of the brush, there was this little cabin-shack thing. We went inside and Lamar cooked up some hushpuppies and brim. It was actually kind of cool. I got a chance to sit down and smoke a cigar and do what all outdoorsmen do—you know, talk about how great we all are.

Once darkness fell, it was time to go frog giggin', where you spear the frog, then cook it up on a skewer. And, yes, that's right, I have never done frog gigging before. Now, let me explain this to you. It's about one o'clock in the morning, and we have been out there since 6:00 the morning before, and if you thought I was freaked out about the gators when the sun was out, you'd better believe I was freaked out at night, because that's when all of the gators really make their way out. If you took a flashlight and beamed it across the water, all you saw were red eyes. Those were the gators. Naturally, I had one eye on the frog gigging pole and one eye on the gators. Lamar taught me how to gig for frogs and then we ate them. It was now time to wrap up Lamar's tour. It wasn't until about 2:30 in the morning when we headed back to the ramp.

The thing that I liked about this show so much was the fact that I was truly having an experience I had never had before, not to mention the fact that it was a whole lot of fun. One thing that I must tell you before you take up Lamar's tours is to make sure that, on booking, you check the fine print because, as we found out, Lamar's tours are noninclusive.

Panama

Doug Orr received a challenge from a guy in Panama City named John Shyne. His challenge was to have me come down to Panama, which is obviously taking me out of my element, and fish for pea-cock bass. After talking with Doug, I was totally in.

It was December 2005. The weather was hot and steamy. All the Christmas decorations didn't make it any cooler. Christmas decorations when it's ninety degrees, come on!

I was standing in front of the hotel when I looked over to my right and saw a Lincoln Navigator with a Red Sox bumper sticker. I said, "This has to be our boy." At is turned out, it was John's truck. We did the typical meet-and-greet and I could tell this was going to be a fantastic fishing trip.

The next day, we set out to do some peacock bass fishing. Of course, the weather was very, very bad. So, rather than going north to the big water, we went south to the calmer water for the smaller fish. We drove about an hour and a half south down the river channels and came to a river bend. We anchored up and started to fish. The challenge was John's live bait versus my soft plastic bait. I thought that I could catch more fish than him using my little rubber shad bait as opposed to him using live shad.

Let's just say that, after I was down seven fish to none, I cried "uncle" and started using the live bait and, unsurprisingly, started catching fish. The fish were very small peacock bass, but it was still fun. After a few hours of fishing and me climbing to within a few fish of tying the game, John suggested we go deep into the forest and check out Monkey Island. Doug, Ryan, and I looked at each other, kind of shrugged our shoulders, and said, "Okay, whatever you say, John."

As we approached an island I started to hear all these chirping sounds. John explained that when the monkeys hear the motor, they think that they're going to get fed and they come to the wa-terfront. Once we made it to the island, monkeys came from everywhere. You'd hold out a banana in your hand and the mon-key would come up to you and take the banana and start to eat it right in front of you. It was awesome, but very freaky.

After we left the island we went to another cut in the river system where I tied the match. I named the peacock bass Pedro the Peacock. Evidently, it didn't help, because once again John began to run away with it. Ultimately, he caught more fish than me, but we ended up catching about fifty fish that day. The cool part to me was that I wasn't on a lake catching bass. I wasn't in Boston Harbor catching stripers. I was in Panama catching Pedros and feeding the monkeys in the middle of the rain forest. Very cool.

We ended up going out for a big sushi dinner. Of course, because I lost, I paid. We then hit a cigar bar, had a few drinks, and told some great fishing stories. Doug, Ryan, and I wrapped up the night by going to a casino. We sat down around ten o'clock that night. We played blackjack until 5:30 the next morning. I remember looking up at the TV and, on ESPN2, *Beat Charlie Moore* came on. The blackjack dealer, who could barely speak English, said, "Hey, is that you up on the TV?" I said, "Yeah. That's me." His reply, "Well, I hope that you're a better fisherman than you are a poker player." Everyone laughed.

It was almost time to catch our flight. I had lost a lot of money, and same with Ryan and Doug. But Doug was on a bit of a turn for the good. I gave Doug the remainder of my money and for the last four hands he doubled down. It was an unbelievable run. He made back all his money, and mine, and actually made an extra four hundred bucks for himself in the last four hands.

The Panama show was truly a fishing trip of a lifetime. If I was ever asked to do it again, I would definitely go all in.

The *Beat Charlie Moore* Classic

One of the best shows we ever did on ESPN was when we went down to Orlando, Florida. I was vacationing there with my family along with Doug and the crew. We were at Disney World and we decided to do a show. I came up with an idea called the *Beat Charlie Moore* Classic, which was kind of a takeoff on the Bass Masters Classic, which ESPN was televising at the same time.

The setup was that I'd get a call from Blue Dolphin and he'd say, "Charlie Moore, you're going to the Classic." And, of course, I'm real excited and I go, "Oh, my God, I'm going to the Bass Masters Classic, the biggest tournament of all time." But in reality, he just wanted me to go *down* to the Classic, not actually *fish* the Classic.

So, we hook up the boat and head to the Classic and I say, "Okay, I'm Charlie Moore and I'm here to fish the Classic."

"Oh, well, we don't have a Charlie Moore entered in the Classic."

"What do you mean I'm not entered? I got a call to come down to the Classic. Check again."

"I'm sorry, sir, but you actually have to qualify to fish the Classic and I'm afraid you haven't qualified."

Well, I'm a little upset, so I take the boat and the truck, and I decide that I'm going to fish in the next body of water I see.

To this day, I don't know the name of the lake, other than that it was in Kissimmee, Florida. I saw it as we were driving along. We pulled in and found a local guy who happened to know me from the show—turned out he was from Maine, but he lived down there now. Then another guy who lived in the area comes over and he was actually getting ready to go out and fish. So, I'm talking to these guys and I ask them, "What's a good five-fish weight?"

"About thirteen pounds," one of them says.

"Okay. Great. Tell you what. I'm going to have my own Bass Masters Classic. I'll give myself a six-hour tournament. If I catch over thirteen pounds in that time, then I win my own First Annual *Beat Charlie Moore* Classic."

So I get on the water and after an hour and a half, I've got nothing. "Oh my God," I'm thinking, "this is horrible."

Now the other guy that I was down there with, he went off to fish by himself. After about an hour and a half, I bump into him and he says, "What've you got?"

Of course, everything's a challenge, that's what the show is about. But this time, I'm not fishing against anyone, especially him. I'm fishing against myself. And yet, he wants to know how many I've caught.

"None," I said.

"I've got a little one," he said. "It's been really hard today."

"Yeah," I said. He leaves, and I put the Lunker City spanky on, and I skip it way under the dock, and I catch a fish that was a little over four pounds.

"Man, what a beautiful fish!"

At that point, Doug started getting phone calls from the people who'd loaned me their truck and their boat. They wanted both of them back. So, here we're trying to do a TV show and we won't have a boat.

After talking to them, Doug turns around and says, "Look, Charlie, all we're going to get is three hours."

"Three hours! It's supposed to be a six-hour tournament. And I'm supposed to catch thirteen pounds' worth of fish. And all I've got now is one four-pounder. How am I supposed to get the other nine pounds in the hour we've got left?"

Where am I going to get thirteen pounds? I wondered.

A half hour later, with only thirty minutes left, I skip the spanky under another dock and I laid into this friggin' gorilla. Turned out it was nine pounds, two ounces. Caught live on ESPN! So now, I actually had over thirteen pounds on only two fish!

I bumped into the guy again. He said, "I didn't do that well. Caught a couple of small ones, bada bing, bada boom."

"That's great," I said. "I didn't do so bad either. I was out there under three hours and I caught over thirteen pounds of fish."

Three, four months later, I'm back home and that guys starts e-mailing me, probably thinking that I'm going to forget about what happened that day. He writes, "Hey, Charlie, I kicked your butt. I stayed out there and caught like four hundred pounds of fish."

That's the mentality of a bass fisherman. He doesn't realize that, yeah, he might have stayed out there till eight o'clock at night, but I was out there for only two and a half hours. That's how funny these guys are, that's how funny we all are, you know. It's like he's thinking, "I'm going to wait six months and then I'm going to e-mail him—'Remember me? I'm the guy who kicked your butt on that lake when you were out there for five minutes. Remember? Remember?'"

But it turned out to be a great show. We took their boat and truck, and people at the Bass Masters Classic were calling Doug relentlessly because the tractor trailers were there to put the forklift on the truck to bring it back to the Triton dealership. They were hounding the crap out of us. But that's one of my favorite shows because it was the course of events themselves that made the show fun. You couldn't have scripted that.

10

NESN Celebrity Guests

People sometimes say that, once we started getting celebrities for the show, it began to become successful. That's not true. Celebrities were only a part of the recipe for success. In fact, I believe it was actually the total mind-set of the show that made the difference. Some shows are very celebrity-driven and it's very important that we have that element because people like it. But what some people forget is that I have the same approach with everyone, whether it's the mailman or a celebrity. I don't treat people different because it's Drew Bledsoe or Mitt Romney. I think that's one of the reasons that people started to really like me and the show. I make fun of them. I trade jokes with them. I act the same way with them as I would with a buddy I was going fishing with. This is what became the mind-set for the show, not the celebrity himself. What made people want to watch and what made them come back week after week, was the overall makeup of the show. It had and has nothing to do with whether or not I caught a fish. No. It's all about what happens to me when I'm on that boat, on that lake, either by myself or with someone else. This is what makes for compelling TV.

Anybody can try to get an entertainer to come on their show. But is that going to make it a hit? Is that going to necessarily make it a great show? No. It's the interaction between the two people, it's the way you pull it off, it's whether or not people like you. People get accustomed to being with you every week, and seeing what you're going to do, what you're going to say. We don't have a celebrity every single week and yet the shows can still be great.

But I will admit that having on celebrities does always add an extra element to the mix. It is fun to have someone who's familiar to the audience to work off, to have fun with, to make fun of. And so, some of my most memorable shows have been with celebrities, many of whom I admire. Over the years, I've had athletes, actors, musicians, and politicians. I can't possibly choose the best shows, but here are some of my favorites, along with some of the stuff that you didn't see on the screen.

Drew Blue

One day, I was talking with my pal, Todd Rucci, who was a linebacker for the New England Patriots.

"You know, Charlie," he said, "you ought to get Drew on the show."

At the time, Drew Bledsoe was the starting quarterback for the Pats and I would have killed for the chance to get him on the show, but I'd never thought I had a shot at him.

"Yeah, great idea, Todd," I replied. "But how am I going to do that?"

"No problem, Charlie. I'll talk to him about it." Todd had already been a guest on the show and we'd had a great time. So, together with Scott Zolak, who was the backup quarterback for the Pats, they approached Drew with the idea of coming on the show. A day or two later, I got a call from Todd.

"Okay, Charlie, Drew'll do the show, but he wants you to know that although his brother Adam fishes, he doesn't."

From left to right: Me, NFL quarterback Drew Bledsoe, NFL lineman Todd Rucci, and Doug Orr shooting the ESPN show.

"Well then, forget about it, bro. I don't want him on the show if he doesn't know what he's doing."

Todd called Drew back.

"Charlie says you don't fish so there's no point going on his show."

"The hell with that," Drew said. "I'm going. And I'm going to fish like he's never seen anyone fish before."

Todd called me back and told me what Drew said. It wasn't like I was trying to insult him or anything. I just didn't think it would be too cool for the show to have a guy on who didn't know a rod from a reel, if you know what I mean. But Drew's a real competitor and I guess once I told him he couldn't be on the show, that's all he could think about: coming on and showing me up. As if he could.

I decided to take him and Todd up to Lake Winnipesaukee.

Unfortunately, the day we chose happened to be the day the fish were just coming off spawning, which meant they were just coming off laying their eggs and being in the nest for a long period of time, which made fishing a little tough. I worked real hard to find them, but no luck. When I was able to finally find a few, they just wouldn't bite. You could sight fish, but they weren't going for the line. It was like they were out there giving us the finger.

For some people, that's a sport, but on a fishing show you're actually supposed to catch 'em, not just watch 'em flip you off.

You tell someone like Drew, someone who spends his entire life competing, that he can't do something and he's going to work ten times harder than anyone else to get it done. And that's just what he did. Finally, he hooked into a fish. Practically his first time out there and he scored. But I took a closer look at him and saw that he was reeling it in the wrong way.

"Dude, you've never seen this done on TV?"

He gave me a blank look.

"Are you a righty or lefty?"

"Righty."

"Well, hold on a second. Drew."

So, I went over to him and I changed the fishing handle to the opposite side—and all this was happening while we were still filming, by the way. Okay, maybe it was my bad, because I hadn't shown him how to do it. But the truth was, this was the first time we'd even come close to catching a fish, so I had nothing to show him on. But once I did teach him what to do, he caught on immediately and worked really hard at it.

The thing that always strikes me about these athletes is that they work very hard to be really great fishermen for that period of time that we're out there and, in the end, I gotta say, a lot of them get hooked, no pun intended, on the sport.

————

Okay. Wait a second. I'll finish this story right after I light up a cigar. This is a nine-dollar cigar, by the way. Back in the day, when I smoked in the backwoods, it was two bucks for nine of them. Now, it's a little different. I have one of these first thing in the morning when I get up. I don't wait till the end of the day. It's my victory cigar. I know, Red Auerbach smoked 'em when he knew the Celtics had put the game away. But I figure, why not smoke 'em in the morning in anticipation of victory?

Oh, yeah, back to Drew.
Well, we're out there on the lake and at one point he said, "I gotta go to the bathroom."

"You know, Drew," I said, "you can't take a leak in the lake. The same way you're not supposed to pee on the field at Foxboro."

Of course, even as I was telling Drew he couldn't pee in the lake, I was wondering who the hell made up that rule. After all, where do the fish go? My pee is going to ruin the whole lake?

So, being the genius I am, and seeing that Drew was a guest on my boat and I ought to see to all his needs, I said, "Listen, Drew, tell you what you do. Pee off the back of the boat. This way, if anyone comes along, it's like you're not peeing into the lake, you're peeing into my boat."

As Drew headed to the back of the boat, I went back to fishing. Now, at this point, let me say that whenever we fish somewhere there are always a lot of people trying to find out where we're launching from—think of them as paparazzi—so we always try to keep our location top secret. Because, if we don't, people who know who we are recognize the boat from TV and come over to talk to us, and that can get in the way.

That day, though, word had obviously gotten out, so there were a couple of media boats trying to get shots of us. But we knew they were out there so we were pretty much able to elude them the entire day.

Drew was back there taking a pee just as we came around the point. And there, right there in front of us, is a huge dayliner with all these guys standing around with cameras aimed right in our direction. And there was Drew in the back of the boat and he's got his friggin' pants down around his knees, taking a leak. He looked up and saw all these folks and he turned white. It's like, you wait eight hours and you finally go and it's like the choir is at the front of the boat. My bad. And I was sure Drew was thinking, "Any other time, folks, except when my pants are around my ankles and I'm taking a leak on Charlie Moore's boat."

We laughed about it and, as a matter of fact, I have a picture in my photo album of Drew, kind of in shock, pulling his pants up. I'd show it to you, but I wouldn't want to embarrass Drew any more than he already was and besides, I figure if things get tough I can always put it up on eBay and make a few extra bucks.

During the day, Drew talked about his career, including the trouble he was having with his coach, Bill Parcells. Listen, I never, ever have the intent of making people uncomfortable on my show. I'm not Geraldo Rivera. I'm not trying to get my ass kicked, or kick someone else's ass, or trying to get a story that's going to break news. I'm not interested in that kind of media attention. I'm just trying to have a good time, be a little bit of an entertainer as well as catch a few fish and along the way ask some questions that I want the answers to. So, I wasn't out there looking to shake things up, to provoke any controversy.

But Drew kept talking about Parcells. At the time, it came as no surprise to anybody that Bill was really getting on Drew's nerves. Bill has that ability to ride people and so, as a Pats fan, I asked Drew, as gently as I could, "Hey, how's your relationship with Bill Parcells, bro? What's going on?"

At the time I asked the question I was smoking a cigar—just like I am now—which I'd just put down to do the interview. But just as I asked Drew the question, Todd gave him a big dip of chew. Drew took it, popped in his mouth and, in answer to my question, he goes, "I like Bill. He's an excellent guy." Then he spits.

So let's review. I ask the question. Drew says "He's an excellent guy," then spits out a wad of tobacco. So, my friends, it looks like he doesn't mean a word of what he's just said. He didn't mean it to come out that way, it just did. We couldn't cut that out in the editing room, because it was right in the middle of his answer, so we aired it just like that, which turned out to be pretty funny.

Drew's a pretty laid-back guy and we all knew that Bill could be full of piss and vinegar and in your face so, even though Drew said "Everything's cool," you could just tell that there were problems and you knew that it wouldn't be pretty long before they'd go their separate ways. And sure enough, after that season they did just that.

Our little fishing trip wound up getting a good amount of press. We even got on the cover of *Laker Magazine*: "Charlie Moore and Drew Bledsoe Tackle the Big Lake Winnipesaukee." And there's a big picture of me and Drew on the front cover. Did I say Charlie Moore and Drew Bledsoe? Yeah, right! Let's make that Drew Bledsoe and Charlie Moore. That would probably be the way the magazine editors and everyone else saw it. But to me, it was Charlie Moore and Drew Bledsoe.

To this day, it's the only magazine cover I've ever been on, and I still have it framed in my office.

You're My Hero, Charlie Moore: Bobby Orr

Bobby Orr, who is one of the greatest hockey players in the history of the game, was always one of my heroes. But when I met him it turned out that instead of me being the fawning fan, all Bobby could talk about was how much he loved the show and

Me, Drew Bledsoe, and Eric Sharmer (2000).

how thankful he was that I'd asked him to be on it. Talk about the Bizarro World. It was me who should have been thanking him for all the times I watched him play and for all he did for the game, not the other way around. So, I was kind of taken aback—can you imagine me, Charlie Moore, speechless?

Nah. That could never happen. But you know, people say that kind of thing all the time—how they watch the show and how great they think it is. So, after a while, you kind of get used to it—though you never take it for granted. Never. But you don't expect it from someone like Bobby Orr, who's a legend. But there he was, ticking off at least ten episodes of mine in ten seconds, and all I could get out of my mouth was, "Wow!" Pretty lame, huh? As it turned out, working with Bobby was well worth the wait it took in getting him on the show.

We had an absolutely beautiful day on Martha's Vineyard. The water was flatter than flat. I had taken a thirty-three-foot sailfish boat out and sponsors like Drew Dominic came in from Gloucester and drove down to Martha's Vineyard, which is a long ride to deliver a boat. So, we had this beautiful, brand-new boat, and we were just ready to go. The seas were calm that day, my friend.

"Hey," the water seemed to say. "You worked so hard to hook Bobby Orr up for a show, I'm going to throw you a bone and take care of you."

Before we headed out, I made Bobby wipe down the boat, thinking that he'd hate it and I'd get under his skin. But for some strange reason, Bobby really got a charge out of that. As he was wiping it down, he looked up at the camera and announced, "I'm with Charlie Moore and we're here on the Charlie Moore show and he's a real superstar, so he's making me, Bobby Orr, wipe his boat down." And then we jumped right into the opening.

It was a big deal for me, having Bobby on the boat, and I didn't want to screw around, so I contacted Jen Clarke, who's a charter boat captain down in the Vineyard. Jen is married to Lenny Clarke, an actor and comedian with whom I also did a show. He costarred on the sitcom *The Job* with Denis Leary, and now he's on *Rescue Me,* also Leary's show. I wanted to touch base with Jen and see how the fishing was. She said it was great over where she was going to be, so we went over there and right away we started to catch some large stripers.

Bobby and I were joking and laughing—there was great camaraderie between Bobby and me. We just hit it off, as I do with most of the guys, and hockey players are among the best because they are genuine people who love the outdoors. Maybe that's because they're from Canada and there's plenty of outdoor activities up there and most of them are really into hunting and fishing.

While we were out there, Bobby was busting on me and I was busting on him. And to add to the fun, we caught these huge stripers. We were out on the water for a long time and it was truly a great event. I've talked to Bob several times since then and I'm sure we'll hook up at some point and do an ESPN special.

The Spaceman Cometh: Bill Lee

Bill "The Spaceman" Lee pitched for the Boston Red Sox and later for the Montreal Expos. He was known as the "Spaceman" because he was really out there. And, as I learned when he came fishing with us, that's no act.

We taped the show with him up at Lake Seymour in Vermont, not far from where Bill now lives. It was in the middle of nowhere in the middle of the summer, when it was hot as hell. There are no big hotels up there, so we were forced to stay at a local bed-and-breakfast, which was right across the street from the lake.

Have I mentioned that I hate bed-and-breakfasts? No? Well, I do. It's like staying at your Uncle Bob's house, and it's a total crapshoot. You never know what you're going to get. There's always someone around saying something like, "Are you coming down for breakfast?" I'm like, "Look, let's get a couple of things straight. Number one: I don't like talking to people. Number two: I don't even eat breakfast in my own home, okay? I just want to check out. You got me?" I'm just not into the whole friendly "we are love and peace" crap. I'd much rather stay in a Super 8, where no one bothers you.

Anyway, we were getting ready to check out and leave for the shoot when we heard Bill's voice talking to someone downstairs. We came down and Bill was talking to some older gentleman. And even though he could see we were waiting for him, he kept talking. And talking. And talking.

Then, while we're looking at our watches, trying to get him out of there so we can shoot a show, he started talking to the lady who owns the place. Apparently, the house had some sort of connection to Babe Ruth. According to her, there was some Babe Ruth memorabilia in the attic. Like maybe his jockstrap or something. Yeah, like I think the Babe actually stopped there to take a dump in 1909, or something like that. Oh, yeah, I'm positive he took a dump at this lady's house in the middle of nowhere, and now Bill Lee was standing there talking to her all about it.

Meanwhile, all I was trying to do was get a TV show out of this by corralling this beautiful nut who calls himself Spaceman. So, finally, when I saw that Bill was not about to stop of his own accord, I went over to him and said, "Bill, how ya doin'? Listen, the lake's right down the street, how about we go down there and get started?"

"Sure, just a minute. You know, Babe Ruth once stayed here and . . ."

Finally, I was able to get him to get off the Babe Ruth story and out the damn door and we headed down to the lake. We got to the ramp, me, the crew, and Bill, and everyone got in the boat—at least I think everyone got in the boat. John Sloan, who's in charge of the road crew, looked at me and says, "Okay, everything's a go, Boss. Let's get started."

"Great," I said, but then I noticed something.

"Where's Bill?"

Just as I asked that, I heard the sound of a car door slamming. And then I heard a car engine starting up. I looked over and there was Bill sitting in the driver's seat of the car. He rolled down the window.

"I'm going to get an Egg McMuffin. Anybody want anything?"

"Oh my God," I thought, "what the hell is going on?" Every bass fisherman knows you have to actually get on the water to catch some fish . . . and it's a lot easier to catch fish when you're actually on the boat. Frankly, I was nervous enough about getting some fish for the show because I'd never been on this lake before, which meant I didn't know where to start fishing. And here was Bill, our featured player for the day, playing the Happy Wanderer. He was all over the place, except for the place he was supposed to be: on the boat.

But what could I do? The man wanted an Egg McMuffin, so he's going to get a McMuffin. Only thing is, we're in the middle of nowhere, so where's he going to find a McDonald's?

About forty-five minutes later, he reappeared and, I swear to

Bill Lee and me on a NESN shoot.

God, he started telling us how he met a guy from World War II at the restaurant and they got to talking and it seemed the guy knew Bill's father or grandfather or great-great-grandfather, I don't know who. He was going on and on and on, and he would have gone on even further if, finally, we didn't coax him down to the boat, which was literally something like three hours after we'd actually met up at the bed-and-breakfast.

Okay, now we're on the lake. But it was hot, something like ninety-five degrees, and the lake was dead. Every good bass fisherman knows what it's like to have water that's dead calm: the witch's hour. There's no wind. No movement at all. No fish moving.

"Oh, my God," I'm thinking, "I'm on a lake I've never been on before, and I'm completely dying. There's absolutely no help from Mother Nature. There's a good chance that I am not going to catch a fish." And I was just holding my breath, because there was a good chance that if we didn't catch any fish I was going to be staying in that damn bed-and-breakfast for one more night.

And I was not happy about that. No, sir, I was not having any of that. I was going to stay out there till the sun went down, if I had to.

But nothing seemed to bother Bill. In fact, not even the heat seemed to be bothering Bill. He was wearing a heavy flannel shirt and jeans and he refused to take off the shirt, even though I could see that he had some kind of shirt under it.

After riding around a little, we come to this little corner of the lake, it was really like a point, and when we got around it we saw a bunch of rocks, which seemed like a great little area for smallmouth—a point, rocks, shallow to deep water. It was a perfect summertime pattern and so that's where I figured we'd target our search.

I threw out a line and it was going, twitch, twitch, twitch, and then it stopped. And then, all of a sudden, there were like four or five bass that were coming up to the dock, and they got right under the jerk bait and Bill started yelling, "There they are! There they are!"

I throw the bait out.

"Right there," Bill yells. "There they are. That's a good one."

But they wouldn't take the bait. I throw it back out. There's that twitching sound again.

"Oh, man, that's a big one!" Bill shouts.

Finally, I said, "Hey, Bill, will you shut up? I'm not blind. I can see the fish, too. I'm looking at the same friggin' thing you are."

I think Bill had it in his head that maybe it would qualify as us catching a fish if we both just acknowledged the fact that there was a two-pounder in the water. But you actually have to catch the fish in order to do a fishing show. Got that, Bill?

Anyway, we finally caught some fish, but it wasn't easy.

It's always great fun having someone like Bill on the show, because he's never at a loss for words—or stories. For instance, at one point in the afternoon, Bill said to me, "I fish Lake Champlain a lot. I go up by Marot's. I get a canoe and I take off all my clothes and get naked. I get in the boat, I grab a bunch of beers, and then I travel alongside the east wind down by Ticonderoga. That's my day."

"What the hell happens if you get a west wind, Bill?"

"I end up in New York and I go to a bar and I get in a fist-fight," he says.

Later, Bill asked, "Charlie, you know why all the trees lean to the south in Vermont?"

"No, Bill, I don't."

"Because the Yankees suck, that's why."

He had some great Yankee one-liners on the show.

When we finally finished for the day, Bill said to me, "Hey, Charlie, how about you and me go play some baseball?" I knew that Bill stayed in shape, that he still played in a men's league, but the idea of facing Bill Lee was a chance I wasn't going to miss.

"Sure, Bill. I'd love to play some baseball."

"Then let's go."

So we go over to the local ballfield and we find that it's covered with black flies, and I mean black flies everywhere. It was horrific. It was so bad that the cameraman had to keep moving the lens around to scatter them. We even put a special "Thanks to the black flies" in the credits.

Suddenly, Bill says, "I'm ready to go. I even got my uniform on." And he peels off that flannel shirt he was wearing all day and underneath it he's got this 1908 replica game jersey and then he takes off his jeans and under those he's got the baseball pants.

Remember, it's ninety-five degrees and out on the lake it was absolutely oppressive, and there was the Spaceman wearing all this under a flannel shirt and jeans. He had that stuff on all day. It was amazing that he didn't pass out while we were out there on the lake. But he didn't. Not Bill. He was just waiting for the right moment. And here it was.

Out there on the field, he was really competitive. He was the only guy I've done a show with in twelve years of television that actually wasn't doing a skit. He was actually playing baseball with us. He was pitching to me as if he was really trying to get me out. He wasn't going to let up on me just because it was a TV show. He wasn't trying to show me up. He's a competitor. He wants to win. Finally, after humming a few by me or over me or at me, I had to yell out, "Hey, Bill, this is television, bro. Let me hit one." So, he said to the camera, "Here comes a hanging curve." The curve came in, I waited on it, and then I took it out to left field. And believe me, he was pissed.

Bill is a great friend to this day. I saw him a year and a half after the taping of the show and he said to me—and this is a common theme with a lot of the celebrities on the show—"I got more attention out of that show. People are still talking about it. And you know the one thing I keep hearing?"

"What's that, Bill?"

"People think I'm your dad."

"Well, you know, Bill, that could be a possibility—I'm not going to completely rule it out. I guess we could always do a DNA test. But let's just leave it at the fact that we could be related."

I loved Bill because he was genuine. He didn't read from a cue card. He told it like it is. That's the way he played baseball then and that's the way he does it now. Sure, he might have some faults, some things that make him a little bit unique. But don't we all?

The one thing that struck me about Bill Lee is the fact that he was the kind of person who would sit down and have a beer with you, and smoke a cigar with you, and talk about your life. He's very smart. He's got a good heart, and I'm sure we'll do another show with him sometime down the road.

At Least He Didn't Go to the Jets: Adam Vinatieri

At the time I'm writing this book, Adam Vinatieri is an Indianapolis Colt—and frankly, even though they won the Super Bowl in 2007, I gotta tell you, he doesn't look that good in a Colts uniform, if you know what I mean. But at the time we had him on the show he was still kicking field goals, lots of 'em, for the Pats.

I can't vouch for what he's like now since he's defected to the Dark Side, but when Adam was on the show he was a sweetheart of a guy. A couple of weeks prior to being on our show, he'd been on Letterman and they'd gone outside and he'd kicked a couple of field goals. So, we figured we'd raise the bar a little and have him kick field goals off my bass boat.

Now, Adam is a little more reserved than I am—okay, okay, I know what you're thinking: "Charlie, everyone in the world is reserved compared to you!" But he was cool with giving it a try.

And he looked pretty good doing it. Adam's a true sportsman and he really loves to hunt and fish, but I'm sorry, since he moved on to Indianapolis I have not aired that show yet as a rerun and I just don't know if I'll ever be able to do it. Not unless he misses a

Adam Vinatieri and me on a NESN shoot.

big one against the Pats and then—Adam, are you listening?—I
might consider playing the show again.

John, Save Me Some of That Ostrich Jerky, Will Ya?: John Havlicek

One of my heroes growing up was John Havlicek, the Hall of
Fame member of the Boston Celtics in the 1960s and '70s. I was
thrilled to get him on the show. I tried to teach him a few things
about fishing and I found that he had the amazing ability to understand what I was saying to him, but at the same time he ab-
sorbed only what he wanted to hear. But who could blame him?
I never shut up the entire day and John was so damn quiet. Well,
come to think of it, maybe the reason he was so quiet was that I
didn't give him much of a chance to say anything.

But when he did talk, what amazing stories he had to tell. The
thing that stood out during our day of fishing was his love for the
sport. He loved catching smallmouth. He wanted to stay out
there all day. And it wasn't the greatest of days. It was kind of
cold. But it didn't matter to him. He wanted to stay out there and
fish as long as we could. And while we were out there, he told me
this story. There was that famous game when John stole the ball,
the one where the announcer Johnny Most kept screaming, "He
stole the ball! He stole the ball! John Havlicek stole the ball!" And
that made him even more famous than he was.

After the game, Havlicek told me, people ran up to him while
he was still on the parquet, and started ripping the clothes off the
players so they could have it as memorabilia. And they got pieces
of John's shirt.

Twenty-five years later, he's in the airport and this elderly lady
comes up to him and she says to him, "John, I just want to tell you
that I'm a big Celtics fan and I have a piece of your shirt that I
ripped off you the night you stole the ball."

John told me he wanted to hit her, because he was still angry about that. Can you imagine, thousands of people mobbing you, ripping off your clothes—oh, yeah, I try to imagine that at least three times a day. But I don't know. Maybe that's just me. Maybe I'm just weird like that.

Anyway, as much as I was jealous of John's story and as much as he was offended by the experience, we still understood each other. He had all these amazing little stories about Red Auerbach and his cigar and his presence and the respect that all the guys gave him, and the camaraderie on the team. He also talked about the team being a team and not a bunch of individual players. And we talked about all this over some ostrich beef jerky.

That's one of the things about our show: we've got a big beef jerky thing—Uncle Bob's Beef Jerky is my favorite. If we were like the Skipper and Gilligan and we set out on a three-hour cruise, we'd be able to live for three years, at least, with all the jerky we've got stored on that boat. We've got it stashed everywhere. In fact, you come on our boat, or visit us in our hotel room, you'll probably choke on the aroma of jerky and cigar smoke.

But boy, ole "Hondo" really loved that ostrich beef jerky. That bag would be sitting there and I'd look at it. And he'd look at it. It was a little like a Clint Eastwood movie, both of us squinting at that last bag of ostrich jerky. Finally, I'm looking down at that last whip of jerky, I figure I'd play the good host and ask, "You want that?"

And he says, "Yeah."

And I say, "Damn!"

But what the hell are you gonna do? You're not going to take Hondo's last ostrich beef jerky, if you know what I mean. So, I gave it to him, because we're all good sports on the Charlie Moore show. But that ostrich jerky! Man, if you haven't tried it, go out right now. Drop this book—it'll be here when you get back—and get yourself some ostrich beef jerky. Just tell them Charlie Moore and Hondo Havlicek sent you. You'll thank me. Believe me. You will. And then, to thank me even more, you can go out and buy another copy of this book and give it to a friend. That's all the thanks I want.

Playing Through: Coach Jim Calhoun

Peter Gold, who's one of my agents, also represents Jim Calhoun, the incredibly successful coach of the University of Connecticut Huskies, the men's basketball team. One day, Peter called and asked if I'd be interested in shooting a show with Jim for NESN. Without hesitation, I agreed.

Now Jim is a bit along the lines of, oh, let's say, Bobby Knight, the controversial college basketball coach who made a name for himself at Indiana University. You all know Bobby, right? Does flinging a chair across the court sound familiar? Anyway, like Bobby, Jim's very intense, very disciplined, and he likes to do things his way. Sound like someone you know? Exactly. Jim has two National Championships as the head coach and he's pumped out players like Ray Allen and Emeka Okafor, both of whom now star in the NBA. But the question was, could this guy fish?

We would shoot the episode in Connecticut. We arrived at the boat ramp, where I met up with Peter to discuss the plans for the day. A few minutes later, a car pulled up and out jumped Coach with his assistant coach, George. For some reason, George popped out of the car with a nine-iron in his hand. When I looked at them more closely, I saw that they were dressed more for golf than fishing.

After Peter introduced everyone, we launched the boats. We started trolling down the shore and I missed a fish right out of the gate. Immediately, I started losing my mind. Off in the distance, I could hear Peter laughing and yell out, "Go easy, boy. Don't scare Coach." I was thinking to myself, "Wait a minute, I'm going to frighten Jim Calhoun? Uh uh. Who's gonna frighten who today?"

"George," John said. "Look at this guy. He's crazy. He's nuts."

They were laughing at how crazy I was. Now, what I'm going to tell you next is the 100 percent shocking truth of what happened that day. My boat wasn't 150 feet down the shoreline from the boat ramp when Coach said to Bob Sylvester, "Make sure we're back at the ramp by one o'clock, because we've got a two o'clock tee time."

Which might explain the outfits and the nine-iron.

Anybody reading this book who knows anything, and I mean anything, about catching fish, knows that it takes time. Guess how much time I had to do an entire TV fishing show? Three hours.

I went into panic mode. I stopped fishing and took a look at the lake we were on and, like any good fisherman, I picked out the sweet spots on the map. We went right to where I thought that we could definitely catch fish.

And guess what? Coach did. We went out to this point across from the boat ramp and there was a submerged weed line in about ten to fifteen feet of water. We were both throwing Lunker City spankies and we were wacky-rigging them. Imagine that? A couple of wacky guys throwing the wacky rig. Anyway, Coach makes a nice cast into the weed line. I see his line scream off.

"Set the hook," I yell, as if I'm telling him to "take the three, take the three." Are you getting this? I'm yelling at Jim Calhoun. *Yelling.* Hello!

"Set the hook! Coach, set the hook!"

Coach sets the hook and reels up a four-pound largemouth.

Fishing with Jim was truly amazing. To top things off, Bob put one of those floating basketball hoops you normally use in a pool into the lake. Jim and I traded jump shots. But then Jim said, "Why don't we take this to UConn so you can work out with some of the players on the team?"

Of course, I agreed. Let's make this part of the story brief, shall we? Coach treated me just like a regular player. He worked me like an animal, and I didn't do as good as I did with the fishing. Big surprise, huh? After he was done with my workout, he brought me over for an honest evaluation.

"Charlie," he said. "I've had a great time with you, but you need to stick with fishing."

Okay, Who Forgot to Bring the Protective Cup?: Tim Wakefield

Tim Wakefield was a phenomenal guy. He's a hell of an athlete and, like every athlete, he wants to win. He wants to be better than you. Which means he wants to go on TV and catch a bigger fish than you. If it's three pounds, three inches, or three centimeters, it doesn't matter. He just wants to beat you.

My first experience with Tim was at his home near Melbourne, Florida, where he lives with his wife. We went out and caught some redfish. The funny thing is, Tim fishes in the off-season. Meanwhile, I fish all these shows, it's my life, it's what I do, and here he was telling me how to catch fish. It was funny because Tim didn't realize, he pitches 250 days a year like I fish all these shows.

"Hey, Tim, do I tell you how to throw a knuckleball, bro? Come on!"

Anyway, we went down there and after we fished we did some skeet shooting. And when we were finished doing all that, I tried to catch his knuckleball. It was unbelievable. I had no mask on. I had no protective cup and, let's just say, I really need one of those things. Anyway, I get down there and he threw his first pitch and the thing comes in like it's on snow skis and I'm on a toboggan. It was just unbelievable, like someone had a remote control ball. It was going up, down, left, right, it was just moving in all directions at once. I don't know how anyone catches that on a regular basis. It must be really aggravating. I'd sit back there behind home plate with one of those big circus gloves and I still couldn't catch that thing. So, how do you catch it? The answer is, half the time you don't. The thing just friggin' moves.

From left to right: John Martin, Bob Sylvester, Tim Wakefield, and me on a NESN shoot (2002).

"Tim, what're you doing?" I asked him. "I can't catch that thing. Try something else." So, I got back down behind the plate and he threw me a fastball, only this time the ball flew over my head. I mean, these guys are professionals. You don't really understand that until you start playing with them.

The Perfect Hair Day: Mitt Romney

One day, Bob got a call from Governor Mitt Romney's office, but he didn't take it seriously. He thought maybe we were really late on paying our taxes, so late that we were getting a personal call from the governor. When he told me about the call, all I could think was, "Oh, God, what did we do this time? We must have really screwed up. Don't return the call, Bob."

But the governor's office called again, so Bob figured he'd better call back. When he did, he talked to someone named Josh who told him that Mitt and his wife were big fans of the show and that Mitt wanted to be on it. When Bob called me up and told me about it I said, "Great, maybe we can do something really cool. See what he wants to do."

Bob called Josh who said, "You know, the governor's an expert water-skier."

"That's great," said Bob, "Why don't we take Mitt waterskiing behind Charlie's boat."

"Hey, idiot," I said when Bob proposed this idea to me. "Maybe you're not aware of this, but I've never taken anyone waterskiing before off the back of my boat. That might be a little problem, don't you think? I mean, call me crazy, but do you really think that, considering I've never done this before, that the first guinea pig ought to be the governor of the state of Massachusetts?" I paused, and then continued, "Yet, come to think of it, it might not be a bad thing because, if anything happens, it's gonna be all over CNN. . . . Yeah, this is gonna be good, real good."

You see, I'm always looking on the bright side of things. And now, suddenly, this looked like a no-lose proposition.

We worked hard to find the ultimate location. That's what we do with all the guests. We decided on Lake Cochituate in Framingham, Massachusetts, off Route 9, which was convenient for everybody.

There was only one problem. We discovered that you aren't allowed to water-ski on the lake. But wait. That wouldn't be a problem. After all, we were going to be waterskiing with the governor of Massachusetts. He'd have the state police there and a police boat. Who was going to tell the governor that he couldn't ski the lake?

But there was something else bothering me. I didn't know if the insurance was paid on my boat, or if it was even registered. And there were going to be cops everywhere. Suddenly, I was

Mitt Romney and me.

very uncomfortable. What if someone came over and asked me if I had a fishing license? But hold on, if they did, wouldn't that make a great segment?! If someone did ask me for my fishing license, I could just turn around and say, "Uh, maybe you ought to talk to my good friend and fishing partner, Mitt Romney, the *governor of the State of Massachusetts.*"

Mitt turned out to be a phenomenal guy. At the time I'm writing this book, Mitt is running for president. Looking back on it, I think that might have been part of the reason why he wanted to come on my show. I'm serious. By going out fishing with me, a regular guy—and believe me, you don't get any more regular than I am—he could show that he was a regular guy, too. I think he wanted that image.

Anyway, we set things up and, right before we're ready to go out, Mitt, who's in phenomenal shape—he's got the body of a forty-year-old, with perfect hair, which I'm really pissed off about—comes up to me and says, "Charlie, don't go over thirty-five miles an hour."

"Yeah, right. Just get in the lake, bro."

So, he gets in the lake. I gun the engine. In a matter of a few seconds I'm going forty-five and I look back and the governor's hair isn't even moving. Then, he gets up on one slalom ski and he's ripping up the lake. It was unbelievable. Turns out he really is a phenomenal skier.

"Geez," I thought to myself. "All you need to be a politician is, you've gotta be able to say that you never inhaled, and you've gotta have perfect hair."

After he's smoked the lake, Mitt turns to me and says, "Hey, Charlie, you want to give it a try?"

Why let the governor make me look bad on my own show when I can do that all by myself? So I get in with two skis on, obviously, and I couldn't get up to save my rear end. I'd just about get up on the skis when I'd hear the motor go "rrrrrr" and I'm like, "What the hell, give it some gas. Go! Go! Go!"

Of course, I would have gotten up, but I know for a fact that Mitt Romney kept on coming up on the throttle.

Mitt Romney waterskiing.

Let's face it, the governor was trying to make me look bad, because clearly it couldn't possibly have had anything to do with me not being to get up on my own.

Actually, I think it's time to tell the truth, the whole truth, and nothing but the truth. Here's the way it actually happened: Mitt's assistant came over to me and said, "Whatever you do, don't make the governor look bad."

"No problem, bro," I said. "It's all part of the show. We'll make him look good. I won't even get up on the skis. How's that sound? But one thing I need to know and then we have a deal. What kind of hair spray does he use?"

Motor City Madman: Ted Nugent

Over the years, I've done three shows with Ted Nugent: two for NESN and one for ESPN. My favorite was the ESPN show, because it was so edgy.

First of all, can you imagine Charlie Moore, the Mad Fisherman, and Ted Nugent, the Motor City Madman, on the same show? As my cameraman, Eric Scharmer, said when we heard we were going to film the show with Ted, "I don't know who's going to get more words in."

At this point, let me say a few words about Eric. I call him the "psycho cameraman." He's a real daredevil and will do just about anything to get the shot. I've always wanted to put a wig on him and let him do all the dangerous stuff for the show. Like he'd be up on top of the mountain and I'd be down at the bottom, safe and sound. But it hasn't happened yet.

Anyway, we headed out to Michigan in the spring to tape the show, a show that would, as far as I was concerned, be the template for my show for years to come.

Ted was getting ready for his Kiss Tour at the time. Let's establish this fact right off the bat: Ted is crazy. As soon as we walked into his house I looked around and said to Eric, "Just keep the camera rolling, because this thing is going to be going one hundred miles per hour." Why? Because Ted is not only crazy, he's nuts. He's totally out of control.

For one thing, as soon as we walked in the door of his house, his cat jumped up on the table and scared the shit out of us. Ted grabs his nine millimeter and aims it at the cat, so that the little red laser is directly between the cat's eyes. It was so quiet, you could hear a pin drop. I was expecting to see fur flying everywhere. I could see the headline, "Charlie Moore/Nugent Shoot Gone Bad. Ted Nugent Shooting Everything in Sight." Meanwhile, the cat went wild and jumped right off that table, as if he'd been shot.

As soon as we calmed down from the cat incident, I looked around and saw a rhinoceros head on the wall. In fact, there were more dead animals in Ted's house than there are at the natural history museum.

So, that was my first impression of Ted Nugent.

If I say Ted was messed up, I'm saying it because Ted wouldn't mind. That's how messed up he is. The rest of the shoot was spent

Ted Nugent playing for the camera.

with me busting Ted's balls and him busting my balls. Finally, Ted had someone at his level. Someone who could talk as much as he could. Usually, Ted gets 90 percent of the words in. Not with me.

After we got off the lake, we went back to the house and Ted went into the living room and got on his guitar. He was wailing away, really amping it up. I mean, come on, you grow up listening to "Cat Scratch Fever," your brother's got the album, this guy is a rock-and-roll legend. Suddenly, you realize you're in Ted Nugent's house and he's playing "Cat Scratch Fever." It doesn't get any better than that, bro.

I can honestly tell you that 90 percent of what we shot with Ted Nugent, you couldn't air. And the 10 percent we could air, was all shot in the last two days. That's how crazy Ted Nugent is.

When it finally aired, it changed a lot of the outdoors programming, though we were still stuck in the "outdoors show" stage, you know, shooting birds, trees, and with a soundtrack of "outdoors" music. We were nominated for our first Emmy for that show, and we won the Boston/New England Award for Best Sports series.

Here's how Eric Scharmer saw it:

> The Ted Nugent show really put us over the top. We'd had a lot of sports celebrities on the show, but this stepped it up a notch. He was so welcoming and he was such a character. And the coolest thing about it was that up to that point, Charlie was always the guy who was the center of attention, the dominant personality. But with Ted on the show Charlie wasn't necessarily dominant. They were neck and neck. It was great to see, because they played off each other so well. It was kind of like watching a horse race, wondering who was going to come in first. We filmed it at Ted's ranch, in Concord, Michigan. We fished in the morning, did archery midday, and handguns in the afternoon. I remember, Ted pulled out these cannons and they went to a shooting range. They were wearing ear sets and protective glasses, but I wasn't really sure how we were going to get

into the segment. I saw Ted there, through my lens, and even though we weren't necessarily ready, tape was rolling. Ted had a gun in his hand and, for some reason, I started mouthing Clint Eastwood's lines from *Magnum Force*. But before I got too far into it, Ted, who obviously knew the lines by heart and knew exactly where I was going, took over.

"To be honest with you, in all the confusion, I'm not sure whether I fired five or six. Do you feel lucky? Well, do ya, punk?"

And that was our beginning to the segment. And it represented exactly what Charlie's show is all about. For the first couple of years, he had a standard opening and he'd use it, word for word, at the beginning of every show. It got to the point where I'd screw with him and even before he'd get to the lines, I'd be reciting them. Gradually, this changed because Charlie changed. He took the formula he had and played off it. And so, a lot of what we did fed off Charlie's outlandish, crazy behavior.

Ted Nugent judging my aim.

That's where the show lived. That was the foundation. And that took us away from the formula.

Charlie and Ted just hit it off tremendously. In fact, Ted asked Charlie about getting a bass boat and Charlie got one for him. Of course, for Ted it couldn't just be any old bass boat, so Charlie got him one that was zebra-striped.

Lynyrd Skynyrd

I met Rickey Medlocke, of Lynyrd Skynyrd, through Ted Nugent. I spoke to Rickey on the phone a few times, and we built up a relationship. We finally connected when Lynyrd Skynyrd came to perform in New Hampshire at Meadow Brook Farms .

Doug Orr and Lynyrd Skynyrd's Rickey
Medlocke on an ESPN shoot.

in Gilford. We put together a cool skit where I didn't have a ticket so I had to sneak in backstage. I get caught and they bring me to the band, and Rickey says, "You don't have a ticket, huh?"

"Nope. But listen, how about I take you guys fishing to repay you for letting me see the show?"

So, we ended up going to Bienville Plantation in Florida with Rickey, an original member of Blackfoot who played with Skynyrd in the early '70s, and Gary Rossington, one of the founding members of the group.

Rickey and I wound up sparking a great friendship. Rickey's a lot like me. He's a phenomenal entertainer with an enormous personality, and I love the guy like a brother. Gary Rossington turned out to be a true gentleman. We sat around the Bienville lodge and he talked about the tragedy of the plane crash that killed Ronnie and other members of the band, which is something I never would have asked him about. But to hear the story from him was just amazing.

Rickey's brother also came along with us, and he's just plain nuts. Near the end of our trip, he came over to me and Rickey with this cooler, and he says to me, "I got something for you, man. Open this up and grab yourself a cold one." So, I open it up and there was a baby alligator in there. I nearly jumped out of my skin. I mean, Moses had nothing on me, man. I parted the entire lake, I ran out of there so quick. Evidently, Rickey's brother had caught it earlier in the day and figured he'd make good use of it.

It turned out to be one of the greatest experiences of my life. It was like living with a rock-and-roll band for a week. I love Skynyrd. I love Ted Nugent. I love classic rock and roll, and one of the best things that ever happened to me was waking up one morning to the band playing "Sweet Home Alabama" in the cabin. It was like, "Am I dreaming or is Lynyrd Skynyrd really playing in my cabin?"

From the top, going left to right: Me, Rickey Medlocke,
Jim Kevlik, John Martin, Gary Rossington, Mike Mattson,
Bob Sylvester, Denny Warren.

Boston Bruins #8: Cam Neely and Other Bruins

By now you've probably figured out that I am a huge Bruins fan.
Being from Boston, there isn't much choice. There's professional
sports all around you. So, I guess you could say I'm a huge sports
fanatic, in general—there's no way I could list my favorite home-
town team. But if I had to put them in order, it would definitely
be the Patriots, Bruins, Red Sox, Celtics, and, of course, my Washington Redskins. Remember, my mom is from D.C. and my dad
is from Virginia.

Over the years, I've done many shows with guys from the
Boston Bruins, like Barry Pederson, Jay Miller, Andy Brickley,
Coach Robbie Ftorek, and Coach Pat Burns. Quick story about
Pat. After the first two days of shooting, we had a big lobster/

clambake at my house in Wolfeboro. Topwater and I were talking to Pat about, you know, hockey, when one of my friends who'd had a bit too much to drink, came up and started telling Pat what players he should be putting in and on what lines. I looked over to the dude and said, "Shut up!" But Pat, who is an unbelievable guy, just let it roll off his back.

And here's a little tidbit for you about Patrice Bergeron. He scored his first goal as a Boston Bruin and he caught his first fish with me. How do you like that?

Fishing with Steve Leach was hilarious. One of the funniest moments of that show was when the camera was tight up on our faces. I asked Steve, "Now Steve, you've played eighteen years in the NHL. Have you had a hard time letting go of the game?"

The camera slowly panned out and Steve said, "Well, it's been okay. I'm okay with it."

At that point, the camera had a full shot of Steve: he was standing on the front of my bass boat wearing ice skates and fishing with a hockey stick.

Funny, funny stuff!

Joe Thornton was another Bruin who went fishing with us. He's a great kid, full of energy, and one hell of a hockey player. I'm still not physically over the Joe Thornton trade. Yeah. Thank you, Mike O'Connell, for quite possibly the worst trade in the last twenty years of sports. And thank goodness he's no longer the GM of the Boston Bruins. Anyway, Joe and I fished on Lake Winni, and every time he hooked a fish, he reeled it in like it was waterskiing, coming in about ninety miles an hour, hitting the side of my Aubuchon boat. He got two minutes for boarding for that.

After fishing, we had a game of hockey. I was kind of pissed that I had to play goalie. Taking an eighty-mile-an-hour slap shot from Joe Thornton: Yeah. That was fun.

I taped a show with Ray Bourque (who was at my Sports Museum induction night), but the show hasn't been completed yet, so I can't say much.

But growing up a Bruins fan, I pretty much loved watching Ray and Cam Neely play. Cam Neely is one of my favorite all-time Bruins players. We decided to go to the Ferncroft in Danvers, Massachusetts. Angela and I were married there on September 1, 1991, but you've heard that story already. Cam and I were going to do some golfing and catch some fish from the golf course. I brought my caddie along, Larry "the Geese" Saggese. Everyone needs a six-foot-four-inch, 250-pound Italian caddie. Pat Gamere was the cameraman that day.

Now, let's just say that I am a much better fisherman than I am a golfer. And this show proved no different. Cam, like Johnny Bucyk and pretty much every other hockey player I know, are phenomenal golfers. I definitely tried hard, but even the magic of TV couldn't make me play a good game of golf that day. Apparently, I was talking too loud on one of the holes. Cam had already told me to be quiet about 452 times. But you know me, I don't know when to keep my mouth shut. So Cam had enough of hearing my voice. After all, he was trying to tee off. So he came over to me and did what any NHL player would do: He playfully smacked me across the face. I fell to the ground, took in a pile of grass, and stumbled back up, and Cam asked, "Are we good?" Me being me, I knew enough to say nothing and the golf game continued without any issues.

Before we started fishing, Cam and I sat down on a rock wall and talked about his career. The thing I really admired most was how passionate he was and still is about the game of hockey. I could tell that he truly misses his playing time. I had to ask him about starring in *Dumb & Dumber* with Jim Carrey. After all, we had a connection. I'm the Mad Fisherman and Cam played a character named Sea Bass.

He told me how fun it was, how much work it was, and how people still talk about it today. After our interview, we went fishing. Cam was all about how to cast. He was all about what lure he had. He was all about learning the retrieve of the lure. He was all about the location of where he was standing. And he was all about catching the first damn fish. We went on to catch several fish from the small ponds on the golf course that day. I'm not sure of how many fish Cam caught, but I think it was around eight.

Sib Hashian Lets His Hair Down. And Man, He's Got Plenty of It.

As you've probably figured out by now, I'm a huge classic rock fan, though I also love rap, country music, and, of course, Frank Sinatra. I grew up listening to bands like Aerosmith, Lynyrd Skynyrd, and Boston. To me, growing up just outside the city of Boston, the group Boston was the epitome of what a good-time rock-and-roll band was. And so, when we got the opportunity to have Boston's drummer, Sib Hashian, on the show, I jumped at the opportunity.

Let's be honest here. The only thing I remember about Sib is his hair. It was the biggest afro you'd ever want to see, the greatest do of all time. I met Sib through my friend, Ernie Boch Jr. Ernie has a rock group called Ernie and the Automatics, and Sib, along with a couple other members of the Boston band, were playing with Ernie.

After meeting Sib, all I can tell you is that he's crazy, but in a good way. He reminds me of myself and, in fact, when I look at Sib I have to ask myself, "Is this the effect I have on people?" The answer is, yes!

I convinced Sib to do a show with me on NESN. We got to the boat ramp that day and Sib showed up with a bottle of whiskey in hand. I said, "No, Sib, we can't have that on board," but in retrospect, I should have said yes, since we had such a difficult day of fishing. We fished forever, or at least it seemed that way, for a total of maybe seven bites, which, fortunately, qualified as a show.

But the best thing was that Sib, who was chomping on a cigar, brought his drum set onto the boat and the fishing got so bad that he actually played a song to the fish to try to get them into the boat.

You know, to me this is what the show is all about. Having fun. Doing crazy, unexpected things. But all I could think about then was that here I was, a fan of Boston since high school, and here's the dude from one of my favorite groups playing the drums on back of my boat. Sometimes, bro, you've really got to pinch yourself to realize just how far you've come.

Sib was a true sweetheart and he had nine million "catch and release" stories about girls backstage. None of which I can talk about now, or else I'll have Sib calling me up.

As I write this book, we haven't aired the show yet, but we've got some great footage of a 1970s rock concert as well as a clip of Sib playing with Ernie and the Automatics when they opened for B. B. King one night.

I just wish Sib had let his hair grow out.

Charlie Catches the Big One: Real Andrews

Over the years, we haven't had too many actors on the show, but when we do it usually turns out to be great fun. One of the guys we wound up having a particularly fun time with was Real Andrews from the soap opera *General Hospital*. We took him down to the P-Arrow Plantation in Alabama. We had driven down with Ted Ancher and Topwater Sloan.

We took the Charlie Moore Tour Bus, which runs on beef jerky, fast food, cigars, and really good music. Often, we have no idea what direction we're going, we're just going. And if you open the door, it's like being in a Cheech and Chong tour bus. Cough. Cough. Cough. Only you're smelling beef jerky and tobacco.

Anyway, it was a long ride and we got up the next morning and put the boat in the water and started fishing. I ended up throwing a fleck spinnerbait. It's my favorite. It was a little different color from the one I usually throw. Because it was a cloudy day, I was going with a shad color, which I got from Herb Reed of Lunker City.

Real Andrews with an eleven-pound bass.

Herb and I had always joked around, asking, "What's Charlie going to do when he catches the big fish?" But in reality, a true fisherman understands one thing: there's no time to play around. You can play around when you're catching the small ones, but when you're catching a big one, there's no joking or dancing around. After you've got him in the boat, well, that's something else.

So, we're down there on the lake and a big one bites my line. Now the average largemouth bass is between two and three pounds. And, if you fish a lot, you might catch one that's five, six, maybe even seven pounds. But this one turned out to be a fourteen-pounder. That's about six or seven times the normal size. I don't know if it was the biggest one ever caught on TV, but it was surely the biggest one I've ever seen caught on TV. And it was definitely the biggest one ever caught on *Charlie Moore Outdoors*. We went down there for a big fish, and we got one. And Real caught an eleven-pounder, so, right there, you have two fish weighing in at twenty-five pounds. To get anything in double digits is very rare.

I was really pretty calm when I caught it, which is the exact opposite of what people would think. I knew it was a trophy fish, so I froze and went into survival mode to make sure I didn't lose him. Because if I had lost that fish, I would never have been able to live with myself. You know.

Fishing's Funnier with Two Comedians: Lenny Clarke

Another Boston native and hugely successful comedian and actor is Lenny Clarke. Lenny starred in his own sitcom, *Lenny,* and

From left to right: Topwater Sloan, Real Andrews, me with a beautiful Larry, Bob Sylvester, and Pat Gamere.

costarred with Denis Leary in both the ABC show *The Job* and FX's *Rescue Me*. He's made several appearances in Hollywood feature films and has also played the father on the Fox sitcom *The Winner*.

Let me take you to the bachelor party of my brother-in-law, Bill Tinkler. It was 1994 and I'd decided to take the boys to a sushi dinner and then to a comedy club called Giggles on Route 1 in Saugus, Massachusetts, which is currently owned by Lenny Clarke's brother. Guess who the comedian was that night? You guessed it: Lenny Clarke.

At the time, I was working in Revere for my father and being on TV hadn't even entered into my small brain yet. But after watching Lenny that night, I was totally blown away by how funny he was. I still remember a few hilarious lines from his act that night, but it's probably not a good idea that I put those in the book.

Fast forward thirteen years. I got the opportunity to go to Martha's Vineyard and do a show with the great Lenny Clarke. Once we arrived in the Vineyard, the plan was to hook up with Lenny at a local nightclub. Bob Sylvester, Eric Scharmer, and I were all going to take in a show with Jen Clarke, who is Lenny's wife and a musician. Lenny got up on stage and introduced his wife, who, by the way, is an unbelievable fishing guide down on the Vineyard. Yes, that was my plan: Let Jen be the guide the next day, lead us to the fish, while Lenny and I sit back, smoke about forty-six cigars, and tell a bunch of jokes that no one really gets but us.

After Jen wrapped up her awesome performance, we all jumped into Lenny's Cadillac Escalade. Lenny leaned over and handed me a cigar. We both lit one up. Then Lenny pulled the cigar out of his mouth, turned to me and said, "Hey, Charlie, what do you think of the lead singer? I'm sleeping with her."

Welcome to the Lenny Clarke show.

The ride home was basically Lenny and I telling jokes to each other and laughing our heads off. At this point no one was funnier than Lenny and me. Just ask us.

The next day we all got up early—way too early—and headed

out to do some fishing. I have to give it up to Jen. She really knows how to catch those big striped bass down in the Vineyard area. Helping out with the camera boat was none other than Boston Bruins bad boy, Jay Miller. Jay has a beautiful forty-six-foot Intrepid boat, and he's basically as loud as Lenny and I. So here we have Lenny, me, and Jay Miller all screaming during the course of the day. No wonder the fishing was so tough.

And it was tough. But Jen took us to a couple of secret spots near the end of the day, and Lenny and I managed to catch a bunch of fish. I enjoy these shows very much because as far as the fishing aspect of it goes, I view it like this: I'm taking a guy who is known for TV, comedy, and acting onto the show and bringing in a whole new audience that, hopefully, will try and eventually love the sport of fishing. To me, it's very easy to get a bass fisherman to watch any fishing show. But it's difficult to get someone who doesn't know anything about fishing to watch a fishing show. That's where I think *Charlie Moore Outdoors* and *Beat Charlie Moore* have truly made an impact on the sport.

Lenny Clarke is not a professional fisherman, but after this show aired, the response I received was truly amazing. To top things off, Lenny, being the true entertainer he is, said, "Charlie, you make this fishing thing look so easy. Why don't you come to my brother's place, Giggles, and let's see if you can make the comedy thing look easy, too."

So, a few weeks later, Lenny and I were backstage waiting to go on. Lenny said to me, "Let me go out there and warm them up for you." He went out to a standing ovation of about three hundred-plus people and he explained the concept of what we were about to film. After all, we were doing the ending to the Lenny Clarke show. And here's what Lenny said, "I recently went fishing with Charlie Moore. He makes fishing look so easy. I said, I bet you can't do stand-up comedy. So, folks, I'm gonna introduce Charlie Moore, and he's gonna come on stage and say a few jokes that suck, and I want you to just stare at him and don't make a move."

I went out on stage, and really lit it up. I had so much fun telling my jokes and the people were laughing so hard that we were actually dying. Bob Sylvester actually had to stand up and tell the audience to please be quiet and don't laugh. And that's exactly what you saw at the end of the show. To sum things up, the Lenny Clarke show wasn't about teaching people how to fish, it was about teaching people how to have fun doing something you love.

It's a Bird. It's a Plane. No, Wait. It's the Classic Batman: Adam West

I'd heard that Adam West, who played Batman on television, lived along the Fishkill River in Idaho, and that he liked to fish. I asked Bob to try to get a hold of him and invite him on the show. When he finally got in touch with Adam, he found that, coincidentally, he was coming out to Massachusetts to do an autograph signing. The only problem was, he was doing it in November, just before Thanksgiving, when it was cold, which might make the shoot more difficult.

Adam wanted to go to Squam Lake up in New Hampshire because it's where they filmed most of *On Golden Pond*. It's a gorgeous lake, lined with trees—Larry David, of *Curb Your Enthusiasm,* has a house there.

I wasn't going to go up to Squam Lake and blindly try to catch fish, so the first thing I did was call up my friend, Steve Lucarelli, who has a guide service up in New Hampshire. Steve knows how to catch these cold-weather smallmouth, so I asked him to pre-fish the lake, just to give me an idea of what was going on up there. It paid off, because when Adam and I got up there we caught some fish. We also had a lot of fun. Adam West is one funny dude. In fact, his jokes were funnier than mine. And his stories were truly amazing. I didn't get to ask him all the questions I wanted to, but that's because it was a pretty busy day.

I did find out a few interesting things about him though. For instance, early in his career he played with the Three Stooges.

"What was that like?" I asked him.

"What do you think it would be like?" he said.

"Just answer the question," I replied.

Of course, he talked about the *Batman* show, which was one of the first shows where they used computer-generated graphics. I asked him how come they sped up the car when it was coming out of the cave.

"Well, they made the cave entrance a little too small, so the car would only squeeze out of there, which meant we couldn't get a lot of shots of it coming out of there smoothly. So, we did one shot of driving out and we used that every time we needed to show the Batmobile leaving the Batcave. And we sped it up because we could never really speed it out of there because of the tight squeeze."

Adam told me about when he was on the cover of *Life* magazine, but all I wanted to know was how each Catwoman was. Eartha Kitt? Lee Meriwether? Needless to say, we didn't air that conversation on the show.

Adam also talked about how he was on top of the world when he was doing that show, but what I was really interested in talking to him about was how it affected the rest of his career. I talked to him about the Mad Fisherman character, which isn't really a character, it's just me. But to a lot of people, it is a character, and as a result I don't think people have taken me seriously as far as acting, comedy, or entertainment. Where do you think the jokes are coming from? Why do you think a lot of people are watching the show?

The mainstream media tries to act like I'm not an actor, entertainer, or comedian. Like I'm just a fisherman. I talked to Adam about people who said, "Oh, well, he can only play Batman." It was very difficult for him, he told me.

"That's the way it is, Charlie. People are always going to think of Sean Connery as 007. When you do a character and you do it well, people are always going to know you as that character and it's hard to break free from that mold."

When the show wrapped up, we were about to head back to the ramp. There were three boats in total: my Aubuchon Hardware boat, the second Aubuchon Hardware boat driven by Topwater Sloan, and Steve's boat. Now Steve knows that I like to go 172 miles per hour and he warned me, "Don't forget about that submerged rock pile near the ramp." Yeah. You guessed it. On the way in, I hit the top of the rock pile with the bottom of my motor and completely chewed up my prop. Not even Batman could fix my boat after that.

When we finished shooting, and Adam got into the car, after freezing his ass off all day, he said, "Let's see Shatner do that!"

When he got back to his hotel room, he said to Bob, "Here's the number of the car service I always use. Give 'em a call and just make sure I get the big, black stretch limo, Bob."

You know, the one that Batman would use.

Godsmack

One day, I got a call from Ernie Boch Jr.: "Hey, Charlie, Godsmack is playing at the Verizon Center in Manchester. They're opening up for Metallica. Do you want to go?"

Did I want to go? Was he kidding? Godsmack is the hottest rock-and-roll band of our generation. It's what Metallica was to the '80s. And I love Metallica. I grew up with them. I wanted to see both bands.

Ernie and I went to the concert. The best part was when Sully Erna, the lead singer, did a drum duo with Shannon Larkin. They really went at each other and it was very intense. I'm a huge Phil Collins bang-it-and-then-sing-it fan. I love Sib Hashian. They're not one-dimensional. They're very talented musicians.

After their set, Ernie, Bob Sylvester and I went backstage. We didn't know anybody in the band, but they invited us back there

Adam West, the classic Batman, and me
on a NESN shoot (2002).

along with a bunch of their friends who were also at the show. And you know what, they started talking about me and my show. It's a thin line I sometimes have to walk, because it wasn't really my place to talk about me or my show. But I was pretty knocked out that they knew who I was.

I met Robbie Merrill, bassist. He walked up to me and said, "I know you. You're that friggin' wacko on TV."

"Yeah," I said, "that's me."

We hit it off right away. We talked about the concert, about Metallica, what he was doing, what he liked to do when it came to the outdoors. Here he'd just gotten off a huge concert and all he wanted to do was talk about his hobbies. It happens all the time and it never fails to amaze me.

Anyway, Robbie told me he loved to do motocross, and that

he'd actually built a track at his house. Ironically, it turned out he lived right around the corner from me and I never even knew it.

Then, Robbie introduced me to Sully and he talked about his hobby, which happened to be collecting old-fashioned machine guns. We talked about that and then we talked about all getting together to do a show. Meanwhile, I'm thinking, if we do, we aren't going to be doing anything fishing-wise. Let's just do an outdoor show that doesn't even have fishing—a different style of show.

At that point, Metallica was starting to go on and so we left. Hey, I wasn't going to miss Metallica.

A while later, we hooked up with Robbie and his manager and we set up a shoot at Robbie's house. We rode bikes and did an *MTV Cribs* kind of show. Actually, MTV had asked Robbie to do it for them, but he refused. He let me do it because my show was different and because we were now friends.

I rode as a kid, but when we got out there, I was really rusty and, besides, I wasn't using my own bike. We rode 'em hard. At one point our cameraman, Eric Scharmer, Daredevil Cameraman, tried a shot that was, shall we say, a little too much. As Robbie was going around the track, Eric decided to get under the jump. I'm watching and it's like I'm looking at a train wreck just waiting to happen. On the one hand, you want to say, "No, stop!" On the other hand, you want to see what happens. Anyway, just as Robbie's about to reach the high point of the mound, he sees Eric there and Robbie goes airborne, clears Eric, thank God, and it turned out to be an extremely good shot. Scary, but good.

The next day we all went out to Pelham Rod and Gun Club, where we shot some machine guns and submachine guns; some guns were worth ten thousand dollars. For that moment in time, Sully and I were the biggest, baddest gangsters around. We would have taken out "Whitey" Bulger. It was so much fun.

Sully topped the day off with an acoustic version of "Running Blind," and that's how we ended the show.

The whole thing was so quick and so fast. It was everything that I'd been telling Bob I wanted all along. It was like adding paprika to the show. And all of this came about because of the ESPN show, because of the way Doug and I clicked in terms of how we envisioned the show being. We needed to step it up a notch on the NESN show and with this Godsmack episode that's just what we did.

The Godsmack show was the first show we did for NESN that had a lot of similarity to *Beat Charlie Moore*. The first time we pushed it up a notch was a few years earlier, when we did the Ted Nugent show, and that won us an Emmy Award. And now, three years later, we had the Godsmack show, which again won us an Emmy. For me, both these shows were turning points, because they represented the creative steps I was taking in the production of outdoors shows.

ESPN Celebrity Guests

That's a Rap: Chuck Woolery

For many years, I would watch Chuck Woolery on the *Love Connection* and all the other game shows he's hosted, but never in my wildest imagination did I ever think I'd be sharing the same stage with Chuck himself.

One day, I was sitting at home with my middle son, Nikolas, who, by the way, is going to steal his father's job one day—remember what I said about natural talent? Well, he's got it—and we were watching the Game Show Network. On came this new show called *Lingo*. In the beginning of the show, there was a small clip of Chuck Woolery catching a bass. Of course that got my mind going; that little lightbulb popped on in my head. I called one of my agents, Peter Gold, and told him about Chuck's love for fishing. We both talked about it for a while and then moved on.

About a week later, I got a call from Peter saying that he'd bumped into a friend who knew Chuck and that, as it turned out, Chuck loved my show and had even sent in a challenge to fish

Nikolas and me on Lake Arrowhead
in Limerick, Maine.

against me on *Beat Charlie Moore.* Immediately, I called my producer, Doug Orr, and told him about the challenge.

"That sounds really fun," Doug said. "I saw him on the QVC
network pimping his lure called the motolure. But if you're going to do a show with Chuck, you'll have to beat him using his
own lure."

Honestly, I really didn't care. I just wanted the opportunity to
do a great show with Chuck. Win, lose, or draw, it's really not
about what lure I have to use. It's about the experience.

We decided to pick a small lake in Michigan to film this
episode, which would air as one of twelve episodes for Season
Two of *Beat Charlie Moore.* We arrived in Michigan, got to the
hotel, checked in, and then met at the restaurant inside the hotel.
Chuck was with his girlfriend, who was about twenty years

younger than him. I talked to Chuck about his TV career and all he's accomplished throughout his years as an entertainer.

For instance, I was unaware at the time that he had been the original host of *Wheel of Fortune*. I was also unaware of how perfect his hair was. I kept staring at it. It was amazing because it never seemed to move. Chuck picked up on this.

"Why do you keep staring at my hair?"

"I love your hair," I replied. "It's awesome." At that point, his girlfriend jumped in and told me that she was his personal hairdresser.

I was like, "Okay, now I'm getting the picture."

I could tell that old Chucky boy had something up his sleeve. After all, he's been doing this TV thing for many years. The next morning, we got to the lake and spent about an hour trying to get the boats into the water. Once the boats were in, we started fishing, and the challenge was, whoever caught the most fish wins.

Now, let me stop here and tell you something about my fishing ability. I think any true fisherman will tell you that one of the

Chuck Woolery and me doing karaoke on an ESPN shoot.

most exciting ways to catch fish is topwater fishing. But as the morning progressed, Chuck realized I was very impatient. The fish was coming up, hitting the bait, and I was ripping it out of its mouth before it actually had time to get hooked. Man, was this pissing Chuck off. So, Chuck proceeded to give me a lesson on how to fish his bait properly.

"Chuck," I said, "you need to tone it down. I don't tell you how to host *Lingo*." At that point, I realized that it was game on.

Throughout the day, I got to know Chuck pretty well. I could tell he was a very funny, educated, and all-around great guy—not to mention the fact that he has great hair!

Sorry, about that, I just can't get around it.

I ended up winning with more fish. But again, it wasn't about the actual challenge, or at least that's what I thought.

"Okay, Mad Fisherman," Chuck said. "Looks like you beat me with a couple of fish. But I have another challenge for you."

"Okay, what do you have in mind?"

"Well, why don't we go out tonight and do something a little crazy. You know, spice the show up a little bit."

Without a moment's hesitation, I said, "I'm in."

Big mistake. Chuck had decided that we were going to have a karaoke competition at a local pub in town.

Listen, I know I'm good at a lot of things, but a man has got to know his limitations. But apparently, I don't. And so, we arrived at the pub and I was, to put it mildly, extremely nervous. As the crew started walking through the door, I couldn't help but notice that there were about two hundred people packed into this gig just waiting for Chuck and I to do our thing. Most people in my situation probably would have turned and left, and now I'm thinking that I should've been one of those people. But I wasn't.

The biggest thrill of all was, once I got into the place, a lot of people started coming over and talking about their favorite episode of *Beat Charlie Moore*. That really blew my mind away. But enough about the celebrity thing, it was time to sing. I chose "Staying Alive" by the Bee Gees. Of course, I had the soul train shirt on with the disco chain hanging down on my chest. At this point, I felt like Barry White's got nothing on me. But that all changed once I hit my first note. I gotta tell you, karaoke isn't easy. After I finished, I apologized to the crowd and told them that ESPN would reimburse them for all of their meals.

Now I was done, and maybe I hadn't performed as badly as I'd thought. Besides, it was Chuck's turn. So I took my seat in the front row, and here came Chuck. The lights were dimmed and all of a sudden all the TVs in the place popped on with this custom-made Chuck Woolery rap video called *Totally Stoned*.

Talk about running away with it. At that point I realized my chances of winning this thing were almost as good as Milli Vanilli getting into the Rock and Roll Hall of Fame—ain't gonna happen. Honestly, the video was smoking hot. Chuck was declared the winner, and in true professional form we gave the fans one hell of a send-off. Chuck and I sang, "To All the Girls I Loved Before."

It was wonderful to have the opportunity to do this with Chuck, and he was also nice enough to hang around with me and the crew and all of the fans. As the night progressed, we ate and drank some wine, and that's when it really started to get crazy. Now, we're not very big drinkers on the show or at the Moore house, but we all managed to get a nice little glow going. And when you combine a little buzz with karaoke, well, that might not be such a good thing. I came out of the bathroom and I looked up on stage and there was Doug . . . wait a minute. I'm having a hard time telling this story, because I'm laughing my ass off right now. Anyway, Doug was up there singing "The Humpty Dance," which is a classic rap song from the late '80s.

So Doug started jumping up and down with the mic in his hand. The music stopped and obviously Doug thought the song was over, so he threw the mic down on the floor and kicked over a table. The only problem with this dramatic ending, and it was dramatic, believe me, was that the song wasn't over. The karaoke machine was still playing so Doug dropped down to the floor and started looking for the mic. It was hilarious. Bob, Ryan, and I were in absolute tears, as well as Mark Pelizzoni, who works for Winnercom.

But the night got even better. Doug is a huge Pearl Jam fan. So fast forward about an hour later and Doug decided to belt out three Pearl Jam songs in a row. He had his hands tight to the mic, and he was looking, acting, and thinking like he was Eddie Vedder himself. And believe me, three bottles of wine will do that to a guy. And, if this isn't enough for you, later on Bob grabbed Doug and Ryan, and of course he tried to grab me, but I fought him every step of the way. I was not going anywhere near that stage. But they were. They all jumped up there and together they completely ruined "American Pie."

It was at that point, my friends, that I knew it was time to put an end to the Chuck Woolery show.

"What I Really Wanted to Do Was Play the Accordion:" John Smoltz

When filming began for Season Two of *Beat Charlie Moore,* we headed down to Walt Disney World, in Orlando, Florida. I brought Angela and the kids with us and we were going to meet up with Doug Orr and Ryan Moore from Winnercom. We were all really jacked and not just because we were going on vacation to Disney World, er, I mean, going down to Florida to tape a show.

It was because I was going to get the opportunity to fish with John Smoltz, a future Hall of Famer, a guy I grew up watching on TV, a guy who by that time had pitched for the Atlanta Braves for eighteen seasons. Even to this day it amazes me that I was able to fish with John Smoltz. I mean, I remember talking to my friends about pitching and trading baseball cards and I even had a few John Smoltz cards. And now here I was going to spend two days filming with Smoltzy. Yeah, that's right, Smoltzy, because we're tight. Real tight.

Doug Orr, John Smoltz, and me in Florida.

Before I left for the trip, I talked with Red Sox pitcher Tim Wakefield. Tim got a really good laugh out of the fact that I was going down to Florida to drive John Smoltz crazy. Tim explained just how laid-back John is. But my approach was going to be no different than any other show I've done.

The day before filming we all decided to go to the Magic Kingdom. I was walking around the corner and I bumped into one of the local fishing guides.

"Hey, Charlie," he said, "you're fishing with Smoltz, huh?"

"Yeah. I can't wait."

"Well, you know, John's been on the lake all day pre-fishing with one of the other guides."

I laughed hard. Very hard. But it was no joke, because it gave me my first impression of John: this guy wants to win. For real.

The next morning, we all met in front of the Contemporary Resort. I could not wait to bust up on John about his pre-fishing day. Apparently, John thought that we were fishing in two separate boats.

"Man, you gotta read the fine print," I said. "We're fishing from the same boat, John. Why else do you think I'm visiting Mickey and eating turkey legs the day before while you were trying to find the *secret* spots?"

Anyhow, the taping of this show was so much fun. John truly was a great guest who also happens to be a very, very, very competitive guy. The one question I posed to him during the show that still sticks with me today is what he wanted to be when he was a kid. John told me that he wanted to play accordion. Well, it looks to me like he made the right choice sticking with baseball.

The following day, I took Anthony and Nikolas to the Wild World of Sports complex where the Braves hold their spring training. I got the opportunity to meet Chipper Jones and Marcus Giles, Andrew Jones, and a bunch of other players. My boys were in shock, let me tell ya. And, truly, so was I.

As part of the challenge on the show, we decided to take batting practice in the Atlanta Braves cages. One thing about major league baseball pitchers is that they all think they can do one thing better than each other, and that is bat. John hit, I think, seven for ten and I hit six for ten, or something like that. But honestly, it was the experience that really made the show.

A few months later, John and I did an appearance together on *Cold Pizza* on ESPN2. The funny thing about this interview was that it was via satellite from John's house and John's dog was in the background and it never stopped barking. It was really, really funny. Talking baseball, fishing, and golf those days with John Smoltz is something that I will never forget.

Play Ball!: Tim Wakefield

When you hear "play ball" you think of baseball. Correct? Well, that may be true. But how about Wiffle ball?

Over the last four years of being on ESPN2, not only do we get the opportunity to do some really cool fishing, but we have also had some really cool side challenges, as well. Some of those challenges have consisted of very competitive Wiffle ball games. For example, after fishing with Boston Red Sox pitcher, Tim Wakefield, who is about as competitive as it gets and who wasn't very happy about losing to me—Tim claims I'm the luckiest fisherman in the world—we decided to play a game of Wiffle ball.

We decided to play it right in the hotel parking lot. People came out of their rooms and watched from their balconies as Tim and I dueled it out.

We made the rules up before we started. If it went over the roof or hit the roof it was a home run. If it went into the third-floor balcony, it was a triple. If it went into the second-floor balcony, it was a double. Any shot on the ground or into the first-floor rooms was a single.

This is always the greatest part of the show. No matter how old you are, you're never too old to act like you're a kid again. Tim and I were more excited about the Wiffle ball game then we were about the fishing. And much to my surprise, Tim threw one mean knuckleball with a Wiffle ball.

It was neck and neck until the end. Tim had me by three runs. It was the top of the ninth inning. I did not want to lose, so I worked really hard and made a late-game charge to tie the game up. I popped up for the last out of the inning.

I remember getting out to start the bottom of the inning and in my head I was like, alright Mad Fish, way to come back. I've got a mean curve when it comes to the Wiffle ball, not terribly fast, but just the right amount of speed, more toward the slow curve. That was my money pitch. I wound up and spun the wrist. It was a beautiful pitch. I guess Tim thought so, too, because he completely smashed the ball over the roof of the hotel and he won in the bottom of the ninth inning.

But the best part was when he rounded the bases.

"It felt so good to do that to someone else," Tim said. Because, just a few months before, Tim had given up the game-winning home run to Aaron Boone of the dreaded Yankees in the bottom of the ninth inning. Have I mentioned the fact that the Yankees suck? To interject with a quick note: Tim had an unbelievable season with the Red Sox. It wasn't that Tim did anything wrong, it was just the fact that Boone was lucky as hell. Don't make me start talking about Bucky "F'en" Dent. Talk about making a career off of one hit.

Anyway, back to the story. I was glad to help out Tim with this very therapeutic Wiffle ball game. But one more thing. The following year, the Red Sox went on to beat the Yankees down three games to none for the greatest comeback in sports history. I'm not saying that the Wiffle ball game had anything to do with that. Or am I?

Who Really Won?: Round Two
with Rickey Medlocke

Five or six months after our first fishing trip, in the early spring, Rickey called me up.

"Hey, Charlie, you want to go fishing down in Alabama?"

Yeah, like I was going to say no to that. So, we wound up at a place called the Roost. I brought cameras down with me to personally document the trip, but it actually turned out to be a huge challenge, a true reality event, that we turned into an episode for *Beat Charlie Moore*.

We were staying in these motel-like cabins on the edge of a pond. Rickey suggested that we meet on the pond and just fish the shoreline. Now, I can't prove this, but I think that during the night Rickey came into my room and unplugged my alarm clock. And, being the sleeper that I am, I overslept. By the time I got out there, Rickey had already done two hours' worth of fishing and he had a seven-to-nothing lead on me.

I accused him of pulling the alarm clock stunt but, of course, he didn't admit to anything. In the meantime, I was out there casting my line and, eventually, I caught up with him. Then, I decided to even the score with Rickey. Now, in truth, we didn't need a fishing license because we were on private property, but Rickey didn't know that. So, as soon as he took the lead, I excused myself and made a call to Doug Orr, my ESPN producer, and told him to call the Fish and Game Authority.

Within half an hour, they sent someone over and "arrested" Rickey for fishing without a license. That'll teach him to screw around with the Mad Fisherman.

Round Three: The Mad Fisherman and Rickey Medlocke Versus Three Doors Down

Fast forward another three or four months, it's August now, and I get a call on my cell phone from Rickey. I know it's Rickey before he even says so because his voice is so recognizable. He sounds just like Stephen Tyler.

"Hey, Charlie, it's Rickey Medlocke. How you doin', buddy? Listen, I gotta tell you something right now. I'm backstage with this damn band, Three Doors Down, and we're talking some serious smack, you know what I mean? It's ridiculous, but here's what we're fixing to do. We want to go down to Louisiana, go catch some redfish. We gotta shut these boys up from Three Doors Down. They think they can beat old Medlocke and Moore in a fishing duel. Don't embarrass me, man. Now get down here, and get down here quick!"

So I ended up going down to Venice Marina in Venice, Louisiana, where we hooked up with Rickey and four guys from Three Doors Down: Brad Arnold, Matt Roberts, Todd Harrell, and Chris Henderson. Denny Warren came down with me and brought three Sailfish boats with him, including a custom-made orange *Dukes of Hazzard* boat for me.

The fishing was amazing. It was the year after the hurricane and they were still pretty traumatized down there. It was horrible to see the devastation. It was a true reality check. But the fishing, well, the fishing was just out of control.

We had special rules for the challenge, because, you know, that's what guys do, make up their own rules as they go along. That's what fishing's all about, and it's especially what it's all about if you're doing a TV show like mine. If you caught a catfish, your score would go back down to zero. Of course, this led to a lot of, oh, let's call it what it was: cheating! No one wanted to admit they caught a catfish, so we saw people leaning over and cutting the line if they hooked one.

But probably the best part of the whole show was that we were on this big, beautiful houseboat and Rickey and Three Doors Down start playing each other's songs acoustically. They also started writing songs for their next album. Meanwhile, I'm just sitting there thinking to myself, "Are you kidding me? How can anybody not be having fun right now?"

While Rickey and I were talking about a deal we were working on, Three Doors Down was writing songs for the new album. We were up all night but, hey, I was with a rock band, and I think when they sign the contract it's on page 201, paragraph B, line 1:

Rickey Medlocke, Three Doors Down, and me.

"Up all night." That's par for the course when you're a rock-and-roll band.

The Motor City Madman: Ted Nugent

I took trip to Crawford, Texas, not to visit George W. Bush, but to visit Ted Nugent, who was living down there. I was late and Ted was leaving me all kinds of messages on my cell, which I didn't get because we were going in and out of coverage. But the last thing in the world you want to do is make Ted Nugent wait. If you don't know why, you'll see soon enough. When we finally made it to the place where we were supposed to meet up, we saw Ted peel out of the parking lot and we followed him to his ranch.

Once we got there, we immediately fell into conversation. But as you know from our previous shows, when you're with Ted you have to fight for real estate when it comes to the talking thing. Wherever we are, whomever we're with, we're the two most dynamic people in the room.

Ted has two small ponds on his ranch and that's where we planned to hold the challenge. I love fishing from the shore on TV, though some people think it's kind of stupid. But it's not. It's totally real fishing. Look, not every viewer has a bass boat or a sailfish at his disposal. And when I fished with my father-in-law, Dickie, we went to the pond and talked and cast for three, four hours.

So, Ted and I went to the pond, the challenge being, who would catch the most fish. We were *killing* the fish. I started winning but Ted started doing some very creative accounting. If I had eight fish and he'd catch one, he'd yell out, "I got one. Number ten." And then, if I had ten and he caught one, he'd yell out, "Got another. Number twelve." So, he was counting two fish for every one he caught. And then, when we'd come back from commercial break, he'd announce, "I caught five." Believe me, he never caught five.

But who cared? We were having fun.

The best part of the day, though, was how freaked out Doug Orr got. Doug hates stress. When it starts to come on, he'll grab a bottle of water and a cigarette . . . no, not one cigarette, maybe half a pack. And Ted was freaking him out. Yeah, Ted was out of control again, but in a good way, like me.

Anyway, at one point, Ted grabbed a five-pound bass, but he got away. That happens. But evidently not to Ted, because he grabbed his nine millimeter from his hip and starts firing away into the pond.

"I killed it! I killed it! That's four points for me."

He didn't get it, of course. But that didn't matter to Ted.

Most people's reaction would be, "Okay, we'll get it next time." Not Ted. He blows up the lake.

Meanwhile, Doug was like, "This is not right." Yeah, Doug, we're not in Kansas anymore, bro.

After we finished fishing, we went back to the ranch and shot some stuff there, in Ted's house, and listened to some music. Ted played this very powerful song he wrote about his friend, Fred Baer, who was a tremendous hunter, and he was really getting pretty choked up. When he was done, he started talking about how much Fred meant to him. Stuff like that really blows me away.

We also did a little bit with Ted, called "Ted on Ted," in which Ted Nugent gave his thoughts about our other Ted, Ted Kennedy. Just before the show was about to air, ESPN saw a rough copy and they thought it was much too edgy and over the top, so they made us edit it way down. Apparently, blowing up half the lake was okay, but Ted Nugent talking about Ted Kennedy was a problem.

Rhyming and Reeling with Darryl "DMC" McDaniels

Growing up as a kid in Lynnfield, Massachusetts, I'd spend a lot of time in our backyard playing sports. Of course, playing sports with my brothers inevitably meant we'd end up in a brawl.

But while we played, we'd often bring out a boom box. I'm a huge fan of all kinds of music—I was member of the MTV generation at a time when MTV actually played music videos. One style of music I enjoyed while playing with my brothers was what I called rap and roll, which had a rock-and-roll beat with a little rap twist.

By now you know that I was a big fan of Frank Sinatra, Lynyrd Skynyrd, Ted Nugent, Metallica, and Boston's own Aerosmith. Other acts I enjoyed were the Beastie Boys, LL Cool J, and Eric B. and Rakim. (If you want me to get even more detailed, and I'm sure you do, I'm also a huge, and I mean *huge,* fan of '80s hair metal bands like Mötley Crüe, Ratt, and Judas Priest.)

But out there in the backyard, playing ball with my brothers, I really started getting into this rap and roll music.

You're probably wondering why I'm rambling on about the music I love. Well, one day not too long ago my phone rang. It was Peter Gold.

"Charlie, do you know a band called Run-DMC?"

"Yes, Peter," I said. "I grew up absolutely loving their music."

"Well, apparently DMC is a big fan of the show and wants to be on both shows."

And thus, the stage was set for the Mad Fisherman to fish with Darryl "DMC" McDaniels, which, as you can imagine, I was pretty psyched about.

About a month later, Darryl rolled into town with his agent, Eric, and from that point on it was four days of nonstop filming. The first part of the show would take us to Manchester Harley-Davidson where my good friend Steve Talarico hooked us up with free Harleys to ride on the show. We drove the bikes to a secret location and proceeded to catch plenty of trout. During the shoot, I couldn't help but notice how much he got hooked (no pun intended) into the fishing thing.

"The first thing that I'm going to do when I get home is buy my own rod and reel," he said.

Now, when you get right down to it, when you strip away all the glitz and glamour, this is really the best part of what I do. Whether it's a rock and roller, an actor, or an everyday Joe, getting someone excited about the outdoors is what I love to do. And, believe me, Darryl was hooked. From the moment he got out there on the water, I could tell he was having a great time.

While filming an episode of *Beat Charlie Moore,* I could tell that old Darryl wanted to win. He got on the scoreboard first with one trout. But I soon countered with my very own trout, tying things up one apiece. Darryl struck again with another rainbow trout. I waited a few minutes, turned to Darryl and said, "You up two to one, bro?"

"Yeah," he said, and you could tell he was damn proud of it.

But I flipped my own bait tight to the rocks and quickly tied things up 2–2. This went back and forth for a while and during the fishing I had the privilege of talking with Darryl about his career. Run-DMC, Darryl told me, was a band that accomplished many groundbreaking things: it was the first rap band to be on MTV, the first rap band on the cover of *Rolling Stone;* the first rap band with a shoe contract . . .

At which point I jumped in and said, "first rap band to lose on *Beat Charlie Moore.*"

We laughed over that one (although I was dead serious, of course). But the most interesting part of the conversation was when Darryl was describing how their cover of "Walk This Way" with Aerosmith came about.

"That song helped out both bands," Darryl explained. It was at a time when Aerosmith was making a huge comeback and the music video was a huge success on MTV.

But it was the behind-the-scenes info that really intrigued me. According to Darryl, none of the band members were sure how the song would actually turn out. It wasn't until they heard the track from Steven Tyler and Joe Perry. Once they heard that track, DMC and Run knew they were on to something. And that's how the rap-and-roll version of "Walk This Way" was born. It was a huge success, the very first hip-hop single to make it to *Billboard*'s Top 10.

But back to the fishing, my friends. The next day, we started filming an episode for *Charlie Moore Outdoors*. We got to the ramp where John Leone and Keith Kevlik, who had driven my two Aubuchon boats there, realized we had no place to park the trucks and trailers once we launched the boats. I told John to go across the street and knock on the guy's door and ask if we could park our trucks in his yard. John knocked on the door, and it turned out I actually knew who the guy was. It was a lucky break, because we might not have been able to film the episode with no place to park.

Vehicles parked, we headed out onto Bow Lake. The fishing was, well, how do I say this? Horrible. I worked my butt off for each little fish I caught. But the conversation never stopped. Everybody had a whole bunch of fun because, after all, we were on the water, chilling and catching fish with a music legend. It doesn't get any better than that.

On day three of filming, we were to shoot the music segments for both shows. I called upon my good friend Gary Funchion, who has a band called Dr. Humble, the group that does the theme song for *Charlie Moore Outdoors*. We all met at the Tupelo Music Hall in Londonderry, New Hampshire. Everybody was pumped, to put it mildly. The band was warming up and sounded awesome. Darryl walked into the hall, jumped up on the stage, and they went at it for about half an hour. It was a great warm-up session, let me tell ya. Gary and Darryl got on the same page with the rest of the band and belted out a rap version of the Mad Fisherman theme song. It was awesome! Of course, I couldn't let Darryl upstage me, so I jumped up there and belted out my own rap. It went a little something like this:

> *The final score was four to three*
> *There ain't no way DMC beat me*

Cause I'm the Mad Fisherman of the great outdoors
Yeah, that's right, I'm Charlie Moore
We rode some bikes, then hit the lake
We caught some fish and things were great
Well my friends it's time to go
But I thank you all for watching the show
About rhyming and reeling with DMC
But don't you worry we'll be back next week
'Cause the show is fun, that's what it's all about
For DMC, I'm Mad Fish. Peace. We're out.

For me, this was totally groundbreaking. For years, fishermen have done shows with other fishermen and concentrated on one thing—teaching viewers how to fish *their* way. My shows are all about teaching you how much fun you can have in the great outdoors.

Darryl McDaniels, better known as DMC, was not a fisherman, but after the shows we did together, I think we can now call him one. I will always remember these two episodes, because we pulled off what most shows would never even try to attempt. That's what I'm most proud of.

By the way, I think DMC and I will be doing a rap-and-roll tour next year, so keep on the lookout.

One Last Celebrity Brush with Greatness: Me and Mike O'Malley

It was at the MLB All-Star break in July 2006, and I was going to a charity event hosted by Tim Wakefield and Jason Varitek of the Boston Red Sox. I wasn't feeling well at all. I was run-down from burning the candle at both ends—something new for the Mad Fisherman, right? I told Bob Sylvester I really didn't feel like going, but he convinced me that I had to and so, along with Angela and a few friends, I walked into a Boston comedy club.

Almost immediately, I spotted a man I've wanted to talk to for so many years: comedian Mike O'Malley, who had his own sitcom, *The Mike O'Malley Show,* and costarred on the long-running CBS sitcom *Yes, Dear.* I walked over to him and before I could say anything Mike said, "Finally, we meet."

It turns out that Mike felt the same way about me as I felt about him. We took an instant liking to each other. It felt like we already knew each other. It was like, "Where did we leave off, bro?"

"Listen," Mike said. "We're going to do a little stand-up here. Why don't you come on up?"

You're asking the Mad Fisherman to get in front of a crowd and perform? Do you think I'm going to say no? I wasn't prepared, but that never stopped me before, did it? So, I got up there and I started to lose my mind. It was beastly hot in there, people were laughing, I don't even know what I was saying, and I was like in another zone. Meanwhile, Mike was sitting down on the stage, having a glass of water. In retrospect, I just hope I didn't insult anyone. Finally, I got off the stage, hoping I didn't do anything wrong, and Mike picks up the microphone and says, "And I'll bet you all thought Sam Kinison was dead."

After the event, we talked and exchanged phone numbers. I mentioned to Mike about a show I'd been thinking about for two or three years and he said, "That idea kicks. I can see it."

I thought that would be the end of it, but no. Mike called his agent from CAA, Jeff Jacobs, told him about me, and now the stage is set for something potentially very big—a sitcom of my own.

Mike made that connection for me and it was way, way above and beyond. I won't ever forget that night. And Mike, don't worry, bro, when I get that sitcom—and I will—you'll be making all the guest appearances you want.

12

Death-Defying Tales

Fishing isn't inherently dangerous, unless, of course, you play it a little too fast and loose with your fishing line and hook. But over the years I have found myself in some dangerous situations, most of which could go under the heading of: It sounded like a good idea at the time.

In the beginning, when we had no money to speak of, we had a limited amount of time to shoot each show—we didn't have the money to spend four days at a location, because that would have meant meals and, besides, NESN wasn't going to give the camera to Charlie Moore for more than twenty-four hours.

More often than not, we carpooled. But that "we" is a little misleading, since I didn't even have a car that actually worked. Just that truck, which wasn't big enough to hold all of us. As a result, one of the other members of the crew would usually "volunteer" the use of his car.

Early on—it was probably our first or second season doing *Front Row*—we were driving down from Block Island, where we'd done a night shoot, a striper show. My cameramen Sal and Eric were in the car along with Bob Sylvester and me. It was very late at night, but we had no choice since we had another shoot the next day. Bob and Eric were sleeping, I was half-awake, and Sal was driving. I closed my eyes for what couldn't have been more than a second and evidently Sal chose that very same second to close his eyes. The car began to swerve off the road. For some reason, I woke up and found that I was staring at a telephone pole right in front of me. And it seemed to be getting closer and closer.

"Sal!" I screamed.

Sal slammed on the breaks and we came within inches—and I do mean inches—of that pole.

That might have been all she wrote for Charlie Moore.

The good old days, huh?

Wrestlemania

When I'm tired of doing straight fishing or I think people are tired of watching me fish, we put together a skit. I like the change of pace. It's like all rock and rollers wanting to be actors and all actors wanting to be rock and rollers. Everybody wants to be somebody else. Sometimes I feel like, "Gee, I'm really having a good time with this fishing thing, but I really want to take a break. What do I want to do?"

One time, I just felt like doing some wrestling. Had I ever wrestled? No. But that wasn't going to stop me. And, of course, when I come up with an idea like that, nobody even tries to talk me out of it because they know it's going to make for a good show. That I might get killed or maimed, well, that doesn't matter, so long as it makes for good TV.

So, I found a wrestler—I don't even remember his name, but I do remember he was a very large man—and I got in the ring with him. And, big surprise, he started to beat the crap out of me. Of course, my kids were there, including my daughter, who was pretty young at the time. And when she saw what was going on in the ring, she jumped up, started crying, and shouted, "You're killing my dad. You're killing my dad." Meanwhile, everyone else was laughing. A few people even started counting me out: "One, two, three," and all I can think is, "Okay, Charlie, time to get back to the lake."

Raging Bull

You'd think I would have learned my lesson there in the wrestling arena. But no. I'm always looking to test myself, to try something else or, as one of my friends once remarked "Who does Charlie think he is today?"

One day I must have thought I was a champion boxer—maybe I'd seen *Rocky* one too many times, you think? The answer: get in the ring with Johnny Ruiz, the WBA heavyweight champion of the world, who happened to be from Chelsea, Massachusetts.

Johnny's manager's name was Stony. Stony, no offense, is straight out of the Rocky Balboa days of boxing. In other words, he's certifiably crazy. After we booked the "fight," Bob and I hooked up with Stony, and Bob proceeded to explain the bit.

"Listen, Stony, here's what I want to do for the show. Charlie's going to come over here," he says, pointing to a spot in the ring, "and Johnny's going to be over here . . ." And then he went on to choreograph everything we're going to do, because I definitely did not want to get my ass handed to me. Again. Meanwhile, Stony was just standing there, nodding his head every once in a while—I wasn't even sure he was listening. But his ears sure perked up when Bob said, "And Charlie will throw a punch here, and then throw a punch there—"

"*No!*" Stony yells. "One punch and Charlie goes *down*. Like a fish. *Down!* There will be no boxing. There will be no sparring back and forth. This would never happen in real life." He looks at me. "You're not even a man. You're a shrimp. You're a bean. You're a jellyfish. You're a worthless piece of shit . . ."

I took a look at Johnny and frankly I can't even argue with him. Next to Johnny, I was all that. And more.

It turned out to be a very quick fight. One punch and I was done. In fact, as soon as I saw that punch coming toward me, I was down on the canvas.

Bro, he was the heavyweight champion of the world! What would you do?

I Think I Killed Him

A few years ago, I was asked to appear at a fishing derby. They wanted me to sign some autographs for the kids, say a few words, and I even brought some Mad Fisherman gear to give away. I had a microphone and I was doing a few interviews. At one point, I approached this guy, Peter, who'd set up the whole thing and asked him, "Hey, do you mind if I interview you?"

"Sure."

So, we set up in front of the pond and my cameraman, who has an earpiece in one ear to listen to everything I have to say, starts to film it.

The camera begins to roll and I said, "It's a great day down here and we sure do appreciate you inviting the Mad Fisherman down to share it with you. We've got a lot of kids who've shown up today, so I think it's going to be a great event . . ."

And then I hand the mic over to the guy for him to say a few words, and he just mumbled, "Yeah."

So, I take the mic back and I just go on my merry way.

"The weather's great, and I think we're gonna see a lot of fish being caught today. Do you have a lot of smallmouth and large-mouth bass in this lake?" I shove the mic back in his face.

Another one-word answer I couldn't quite make out.

"Well, Peter, what kind of fish do they have here? Any small-mouth bass?"

And again, I stuck the microphone in his face while I looked at the camera.

"You know," he says, "I'm not feeling too well . . . but the fishing's kinda good . . . I'm feeling a little lightheaded . . . I think I'm going to faint . . ."

At that point, my cameraman Pat Gamere said, "Grab him. He's going to faint."

But I didn't hear him. I was too busy asking questions. I just took the mic back and said, "So you're saying there's a lot of smallmouth in here, are you?"

As I'm talking, all of a sudden, Peter starts to waver. We were on a bit of a hill and suddenly, he fell over, backwards, like a ton of bricks. Boom! He banged his head on the ground and he went right out. At first, I didn't even notice what was happening, except that I did see Pat freaking out.

"I told you he was going to faint," Pat yelled. So, I looked over to my left, where Peter was just a second or two before, and I saw there was no one there. I looked down and there he was, lying there, not moving a muscle, like he's dead.

All I can say is, "Oh my God, I think I just killed a guy."

Meanwhile, the cameraman was giving him mouth-to-mouth while someone called 911 and a paramedic came down and, fortunately, he ended up being okay. I think the heat just got to him. But I can tell you, that was certainly one of the toughest interviews I ever did in my twelve years on TV.

Look in the Sky. Is It a Bird? Is It a Plane?
Wait Minute. Isn't That the Mad Fisherman?

Somehow, the fear of doing something dangerous or downright foolish, always gets trumped by the excitement of getting it on the show. Until it actually happens, that is. Take the time someone came up with the idea of having me go skydiving. It "seemed like a good idea at the time." But once I saw that tiny plane waiting for us on the runway, I wasn't so sure.

The plane was big enough to hold the pilot, the instructor, me, and my cameraman, Eric Scharmer. Bob decided that, since he was the producer, he didn't actually have to go up and risk his life. After all, someone had to be around to edit the film of me falling to my death.

So, after strapping parachutes on, we got on the plane. But it took us an awfully long time to get up there, which was like dying a slow death. Once we did finally get up high enough, and they opened the door and I looked out, oh my God, it was the scariest thing I'd ever seen. But once I did jump out and the chute opened, and I was able to open my eyes and look around, it was pretty fantastic. I looked over and down to my left a bit, and I saw the plane, diving toward the ground. And with good reason. They were trying to beat me down. You see, we only had enough money for one camera, so Eric had to get back down to earth before I did so he could get the shot of me landing. Later, Eric told me that while that plane was headed down, he wished it were him who'd jumped out because it would have been safer. Welcome to the world of low-budget TV.

Here's Eric Scharmer's take on it:

I'm not apprehensive about high places. I'll take the chance to make it happen. I believe, if you can push your own limits, you can push the limits of the creative work you're doing.

Bob came to me one day and said, "We're going to have Charlie jump out of a plane and you're going to shoot him parachuting out of the plan and then landing. So, you'll go up with him, we'll dump him out of the plane, and then you're going to rocket down here, get out of the plane, and shoot Charlie's landing."

"We'd better check with the pilot."

So, we went to the pilot and asked if it'd work and he said, "Yeah, that'll work . . . unless the engine block cracks from the heat generated by the descent."

Well, that was good enough for us.

I'd jumped out before but Charlie hadn't and he was very nervous. I know that when that door opens your reaction inevitably is, "Whoa, I'm really going out of this plane."

But we pulled it off. I got shots of him jumping, in the air, as we descended, and on the ground. But I did learn one thing. Occasionally you'll read about plane malfunctions and eight people with parachutes go down with the plane and die, and you wonder, why didn't they jump out? As I found out, when a plane is going down like that you're literally pinned to the wall. You can't even move when you're in deep descent. I felt like I was glued to the side of the plane, and I was hanging onto my stomach. It felt like we were crashing.

Recently, we did another skydiving show for ESPN, but this time I made everybody, the whole crew, do it with me. So you can see who has more control over the show now. The only thing I won't do is bungee jump. I'll hang glide and do other stuff, but no bungee jumping. I have my limits and that's one of them. I'm afraid of heights like every other warm-blooded American out there.

It's All for a Good Cause. So Eat Up.

You know you've come a long way when you have your own ice cream. I don't even think Tom Brady has his own ice cream

Peter Gold was contacted about a year go by Brigham's Ice Cream—which, by the way, makes the best ice cream in the East. They wanted to develop an ice cream for me. When Peter told me about it, I thought it was a joke and then, when he convinced me that it wasn't, it blew me away.

We kicked around possible names for months, and I finally came up with Charlie Moore's Mad Fish Mud.

Then, of course, we had to come up with the actual ice cream.

Angela and I love coffee ice cream, so that was going to be the base. Brigham's experimented with all kinds of combinations and they sent us samples, which was the best part. Angela, the kids, and I sat around the dining room table, and we did a blind taste test. We'd sit in front of a bowl, take a taste, drink some water, switch seats, take another taste, and so on. When the musical chairs ended, everyone was supposed to run to the one they liked best. I went to number one and everyone else went to number six. Being the marketing genius that I am, I went with six.

Here's the description on the side of the carton, and if you don't find yourself running to the refrigerator to scrounge around for some old carton of ice cream that might be left there, there's something wrong with you:

"Boston's own Charlie Moore, the Mad Fisherman, TV host, ice cream connoisseur. The only thing Charlie enjoys more than reeling in fish after fish is jumping into a bowl of his own Mad Fish Mud with Brigham's coffee ice cream, chocolate-covered caramel cups, and streams of Brigham's fudge sauce. Charlie is donating a hundred percent of his earnings from the sale of this ice cream to help children with AIDS in New England, through the programs at Children's Hospital Boston."

This foundation is very important to me and my family, and I'm very proud of the fact that I've arrived to the extent that someone asked me to develop my own ice cream brand.

And, oh yeah, in case you're wondering, I do get a lifetime supply of Mad Fish Mud for me and my family.

The End? Are You Kidding?
It's Just the Beginning, Bro.

It was truly an amazing night when I was inducted into the New England Sports Museum. And if you thought I was nervous the day before, well, I was a basket case that night.

To begin with, there was that dinner in a private room at Morton's Steakhouse. There were twenty-five of us at an ungodly large table. We had lobster, crab, shrimp, smoked salmon. There were a few toasts. Wine was pouring. My kids were laughing. Sinatra was playing in the background. It was a typical Mad Fish evening.

At one point near the end of the dinner, I called my brother Chris over and said, "Bro, take my credit card and make sure that you let the maitre d' know that I'm paying for all this. It's my gift." Just as I say this to him, I see Ernie Boch Jr. slip out of the room. I turned to Hunter Jim and said, "I know what he's doing. Go after him and make sure that he doesn't pay for this."

A few minutes later, Jim came back and said, "Everything's cool. Ernie said he just had to talk to the maitre d' about something that happened here last week."

Only that turned out to be a lie. Ernie had paid for the entire meal, which just blew my mind because it showed me just how much he cares about me and what I'm doing. I announced it to everyone in the room, because I wanted them to know that Ernie had picked up the tab. It wasn't about the money. No. It was about the respect he was showing me.

When dinner was over, we jumped into the limo and headed to the Boston Garden. When we got there, it was packed with fans. As we made our way to our seats, fans who were there to watch the Bruins yelled out to me, "Charlie, you're bigger than the Bruins." "Charlie, we love you."

By now, the whole evening was surreal, like I was dreaming. It was as if I'd written my own movie script and this is how I wanted it to go; this is what I wanted them to say. And by golly, they were doing it.

I'd gone out and purchased a beautiful cashmere sport jacket, and I had on a nice black shirt under it, and a pair of jeans and Italian shoes. The room started to get hot. I thought, "Oh my God, I'm dying. I started to turn white. I'm going to faint. I'm not like this. I'm the man. I'm the entertainer. This is not me."

Accepting my induction into the
New England Sports Museum.

After Curt Gowdy, Jr., spoke about how much his father loved to fish, how he'd rather be doing that than anything else, I was announced. I had everything I wanted to say in front of me, but then I said nothing. It was too emotional for me. The words slipped from my mind. I had a story to tell about everybody in the room. I had wanted to thank the Gowdy family and the Sports Hall of Fame and the Sports Museum, my family, Bob Sylvester, all the fans, but I got choked up when I mentioned my wife and dad, and never finished the roster.

Somehow, I managed to tell the Harry Sinden and Johnny Bucyk story and, while I did, you could hear a pin drop. The audience was listening to everything I was saying. And then they started laughing.

When it came time to thank my dad, I got very emotional and practically fell off the stage. There's always been that heavy relationship between us because I never felt anything I did was good enough. But my love for my dad is so strong and I know it's because of the psychological drive he instilled in me that has always been a big part of my life.

My mom and sister couldn't be there, but later in the evening, they both called and they were crying on the phone. My mom was upset because she couldn't make it, but she and my sister were very proud of me.

When the ceremony was over, they took us down to the displays—Curt Gowdy's was on the left, in the middle was a statue of Ted Williams holding a salmon and a fly rod, and then to the right, there was me. There were pictures of me and Anthony and Nikolas in their football uniforms with me as their coach, and Kaitlin in her soccer uniform, and of her holding up a fish when we were up in Maine, as well as other photos of me with Lynyrd Skynyrd, Doug, Ryan, and me on our Texas trip.

People started to disperse, shaking my hand, taking pictures with me, saying they loved me and my show. As the crowd started to thin out from in front of the display, Angela said, "Charlie, look at this. Look over here!"

I looked over and there was a whole wall filled with nine huge photos of me. I stood there and almost fainted. My eyes were watering. This is the Boston Garden. Where Larry Bird beat Magic Johnson. Where Bobby Orr, Cam Neely, Bill Russell, Bob Cousy, John Havlicek, and Johnny Bucyk played. And here I am, with a corner all my own. There was the almost life-sized photo of me holding a fourteen-pounder, with the caption, "The Mad Fisherman catches the biggest fish of his life." And there was a photo of me in front of my boat with a Lynyrd Skynyrd one-of-a-kind guitar. There was a shot of me with Heavyweight Champion Johnny Ruiz and his manager, Stony.

Kaitlin, my little soccer star.

And there was a photo of Larry and Stephen Saggese, kids I grew up with. Larry is the Italian Stallion times ten. Huge, wavy, black hair, muscles out to here, bursting out of his shirt. Larry was looking at the picture and he turned around and I could see tears running down his cheeks, so I started to cry. I walked over to him and gave him a hug.

"It's a life-size picture," he said. "I know it's all about you, Charlie, but God, don't I look good?"

It was priceless. No words can ever describe what went on that night.

Later, I got a chance to talk to Mrs. Gowdy, who said to me, "You're so young. It's unbelievable how young you are. Curt loved your enthusiasm, your entertainment skills, what you brought to the table."

I told them my story of meeting Mr. Gowdy in Florida, and what that meant to me. People think I'm loud, I'm full of myself, blah, blah, blah. But I do sit down and listen sometimes. I know when to shut up. I know when to turn it on, I know when to turn it off. I sat down and listened for an hour listening to Gowdy talk. Curt, you invented the sport.

As the night wound down, and the Bruins went into overtime against the Rangers, I was able to sit back and think about the great events that I have shared with my family, my friends, and the sponsors that have helped me along the way, I glanced over to my left and saw the NESN telecast. I saw Andy Brickley and Barry Pederson. Then I glanced over to my right and saw Harry Sinden. And, of course, I couldn't help but glance up into the rafters of the Boston Garden. As I stared at the retired numbers of Number 9 for Johnny Bucyk, Number 77 for Ray Bourque, Number 8 for Cam Neely, and Number 4 for Bobby Orr, I thought to myself:

"Yup. I've fished with all those guys."

My in-laws, Bonnie and Richard Latini.

My brother Chris, me, my sister Julie, my brother David, and my
Dad at the Mad Fish X-mas party (2005).